CATCHING THE LIGHT

MARK LEIPACHER

CATCHING THE LIGHT

Sam Mendes and Simon Russell Beale
A Working Partnership

Foreword by Kevin Spacey

OBERON BOOKS
LONDON

WWW.OBERONBOOKS.COM

First published in 2011 by Oberon Books Ltd
521 Caledonian Road, London N7 9RH
Tel: +44 (0) 20 7607 3637 / Fax: +44 (0) 20 7607 3629
e-mail: info@oberonbooks.com
www.oberonbooks.com

A catalogue record for this book is available from the British Library.

ISBN: 978-1-84002-969-7

Cover design by James Illman

Cover photographs:
Sam Mendes by Brigitte Lacombe
Simon Russell Beale by Charlie Carter

Printed and bound by CPI Group (UK) Ltd, Croydon, CR0 4YY.

CONTENTS

Simon Russell Beale's theatre credits include: for the NT, *London Assurance, Major Barbara, Much Ado About Nothing, The Life of Galileo, The Alchemist, Jumpers* (also US, Tony Award nomination for Best Actor), *Humble Boy, Hamlet* (also US, Evening Standard Award for Best Actor, Critics' Circle Award for Best Shakespearean Performance, Boston Critics' Associate Award for Outstanding Actor in a Large Company), *Battle Royal, Candide* (Olivier Award for Best Actor in a Musical), *Summerfolk, Money, Rosencrantz and Guildenstern are Dead, Volpone* (Olivier Award for Best Supporting Actor); for the RSC, *King Lear, Ghosts, Edward II, The Seagull, The Man of Mode, Restoration*; for the Donmar, *The Philanthropist* (Evening Standard and Critics' Circle Awards for Best Actor). Other theatre includes *Monty Python's Spamalot* (West End and Broadway); *Julius Caesar* (Barbican and International Tour), *Alice in Wonderland* (Royal Opera House). Television includes *Spooks* (BBC), *A Dance to the Music of Time* (Royal Television Society and BAFTA Awards for Best Actor) and *Persuasion*. He is an associate of the National Theatre and an associate artist of the RSC.

Sam Mendes was appointed the Artistic Director of the Minerva, Chichester in 1989 and in 1992 he founded the Donmar Warehouse where he was Artistic Director until 2002. There he directed *Assassins* (Olivier and Evening Standard Awards), *Translations, Cabaret, Glengarry Glen Ross, The Glass Menagerie* (Olivier Award), *Company* (Olivier Award), *Habeas Corpus, The Front Page, The Blue Room, To The Green Fields Beyond*. Other credits include: for the NT, *The Sea, The Rise and Fall of Little Voice* (Evening Standard Award), *The Birthday Party*; for the RSC, *The Alchemist*; in the West End, *The Cherry Orchard* (Critics' Circle Award), *The Plough and the Stars, Kean, London Assurance* and *Oliver!*; for the Bridge Company *As You Like It, The Tempest, Richard III*. Theatre on Broadway includes, as Producer, *The Real Thing, Take Me Out* (Tony Awards), *Shrek: The Musical*; as Director, *The Blue Room, Gypsy, The Vertical Hour, Cabaret* (Tony Award). Film includes *American Beauty* (Academy Awards for Best Director and Best Picture, Golden Globe Award, Director's Guild of America Award), *Road to Perdition, Jarhead, Revolutionary Road, Away We Go* and *Bond 23*. He is the recipient of a Directors' Guild Lifetime Achievement Award and an Olivier Award for Outstanding Achievement in the Theatre. He was awarded a CBE in 2000.

Sam and Simon's collaborations include, for the RSC: *Troilus and Cressida, Richard III* (also UK tour), *The Tempest;* for the NT: *Othello* (also international tour) and the forthcoming *King Lear*; for the Donmar: *Uncle Vanya, Twelfth Night* (also BAM, Evening Standard Awards, Olivier Awards, Critics' Circle Award, Obie Award); for the Bridge Project: *The Cherry Orchard, The Winter's Tale*.

FOREWORD

About a decade ago I called Sam to tell him that I was going to be moving to London to start a theatre company at the Old Vic because I figured that if anybody could talk me out of it, it would be Sam. At that point, he was two years away from leaving his ten-year stay at the Donmar and I was making a ten-year commitment so I thought I'd pump him for information and ask him what I should be looking for and anticipating in running a building, all of which he was very helpful with.

Then, naturally, as any Artistic Director would, I began to woo Sam about coming to do something with us. Those conversations extended themselves for a number of years, in emails and on the phone, in breakfasts in New York and lunches in London. Those discussions led us to the realisation that neither of us was particularly satisfied with the idea that we'd just do one play with each other and then go away. So we began to plan something that was bigger and more long lasting.

What I didn't know was that Joe Melillo at the Brooklyn Academy of Music was also wooing Sam. They had a great relationship because many Donmar productions, including the ones with Simon, had travelled to BAM. One day in New York, about five or six years ago now, Sam proposed doing something between the Old Vic and BAM; this ultimately turned into The Bridge Project.

Through this initiative Sam wanted to achieve several goals: first of all to show that you could bring British and American actors together to do Shakespeare and destroy the myth that it wouldn't work. Secondly to tackle big, epic, classical work with great actors on a large scale. To commit to five productions over three years with a company that exists both at BAM and the Old Vic – its homes – but that travels the world, seemed like a remarkable commitment on Sam's part. He'd spent a number of years in New York and he'd done a number of films but he felt incredibly inspired and challenged by this new company.

Simon's name was mentioned very early on in the process. Sam and Simon have a longstanding relationship and they've worked together many times. We were incredibly pleased that Simon came on board and I think that Simon's involvement was one of the reasons that the other actors came on board: Sinead Cusack and Ethan Hawke and a really incredible company. Simon has that particular core – that pocket of energy – that the greats have on stage. It's very difficult to take your eyes off him because he's such a commanding presence. Yet, some of the moments that are most memorable are the quiet moments: the moments of reflection.

They're an extraordinary team and it's one of those great relationships between an actor and a director, where they've known each other for so long, they trust each other so much, there's a shorthand and a language which they have, there's an ease that they have when they're able to work together. It's one of the great pairings between an actor and a director; it's been the most extraordinary collaboration.

Collaboration is hugely important. Ultimately it's about trust. An actor is always going to be nervous and worried about "can I achieve, can I be daring, can I learn, can I..." There are so many things that you go through that are about having doubt. It's fantastic to have someone in the room that's leading you along, allowing you to flounder and allowing you to discover what the real truth of a scene or a character may be.

I think that one of the things that Sam has that the great directors have is that not only does he know what a great note is but he knows when to give you the note and that's hugely important. Sometimes a director will give a note before an actor can take it or before an actor is ready for it and Sam's timing of when he gives a note is so specific and so valuable and that's a comfort.

None of us are in theatre for the money, that's clear. But when you have someone with leadership and someone in the leadership role, who has the skills and the patience and the vision for what the play should feel and look like it's a wonderful experience. One of Sam's extraordinary strengths is that he's a remarkable visionary, whether in a small space like the Donmar or a big place like the Victorian house at the Old Vic. He fills those spaces with thrilling visual images as well as incredibly strong performances, like Simon's.

I was lucky enough to see both their *Uncle Vanya* and *Twelfth Night* in New York. I didn't see their *Richard III*, which I'm actually quite happy about as I'm about to go into rehearsals for that play with Sam for the final year of The Bridge Project! I did go and see Simon in

Deathtrap in the West End and went for dinner with him afterwards. His greatest piece of advice was "If you have a hump, let the hump do the acting. I didn't, I screwed my body up, I threw my back out and it was a nightmare. Be careful. Whatever you do *be careful*!"

But I'll never forget the night that I flew to Greece to see *The Winter's Tale* at the epic 13,000 capacity auditorium at Epidaurus in the theatre where it all began. There was a beautiful moment when Simon was sitting on a bench, and the lighting was very low and kind of blue, and he was going through an emotional turmoil and he just looked up and his line was "Stars, stars..." and you felt 13,000 people look up to see what he was looking at. It was indeed stars – everywhere. That was to me an example of the power of an actor on stage. He led us up and, without him telling us, we went there. Sam was standing with me and he looked over at me and said "If they hadn't built this place then none of us would have jobs."

Kevin Spacey, April 2011

INTRODUCTION

Collaboration is at the heart of the theatre-making process. Whether the production is a one-man show on the Fringe or a big-budget Broadway musical, each show involves an enormous amount of teamwork. The team may be two or three drama school graduates in their own front room or an army of creative, technical and support staff in a subsidised national theatre, but nobody is going it alone. The working relationships that are formed between actors, directors, musical directors, fight directors, choreographers, set, costume, lighting and sound designers, composers, musicians, technicians and stage managers are the synapses between which each necessary element of the production is passed. Collaboration is a network of creativity.

Perhaps the most intriguing of these relationships to the outside observer is that between the director and the actor. The level of concentrated work, the time spent in each other's company, the different methods they use to communicate, the ways in which they support and challenge one another, are all aspects of a very special dynamic. Arguably, it is this collaboration that has the most impact on the realised productions that people encounter. For plays that feature the large or famous roles, the anticipation for an audience about what they will see is usually directed towards the work that the director and the lead actor have done together.

Writing about theatre is a notoriously difficult enterprise. This 'work' is much more synonymous with 'play,' and like any playground, the games that are devised have their own set of rules and the relationships that develop occur on an individual, person-to-person basis. There is no room for generalisation. The rules are not fixed, they continually change; relationships adjust and evolve. Theatre is a creative art and not a science, and codifying what occurs inside a rehearsal room is often problematic. For the director and the actor, arriving at a performance requires a particular brand of alchemy that is difficult to express in words.

So how does the relationship between a director and an actor begin and how is it cultivated? Why is it cultivated? Why continue to collaborate? Does a short hand develop? What, if any, are the disadvantages? Does creativity stagnate or does work develop more quickly? Does it heighten the quality of the produced work? *Catching the Light* looks at the director-actor partnership of Sam Mendes and Simon Russell Beale – a partnership that has its own set of rules, and its own continually evolving relationship. As such it is not a comprehensive book on collaboration, but offers a window into the extraordinary pathways and processes that are established and nurtured between an actor and a director.

Sam Mendes and Simon Russell Beale have been incredibly open about these processes and their working relationship. I contacted them during their most recent collaboration, *The Cherry Orchard* and *The Winter's Tale* double bill that formed the first phase of The Bridge Project, and since then Sam and Simon have been forthcoming with their recollections through a series of interviews with me over the past two years. Due to their consistently busy schedules, these interviews have always been conducted with them individually, ensuring an interpretation of events from the perspective of either the actor or the director, independent of their collaborator. Their responses have always been open, honest and frank and they speak about each other with a great deal of warmth and humour.

They have been working together for the past two decades. Theirs is an almost unparalleled partnership in contemporary British theatre: a director and an actor both at the pinnacle of their respective fields, each successful in their own independent careers, consistently finding opportunities to collaborate on projects and, in many of these cases, producing their most acclaimed work when doing it together.

Their work over the past twenty years has consisted of eight productions ranging the breadth of the Shakespearean and Chekhovian canons, many of which have toured or transferred to or from the United States, Germany, Poland, Japan, Korea, Hong Kong, China, New Zealand, Australia, Spain, Singapore and Greece amongst others. Their work has been seen in various venues across the UK, not least of all at the Royal Shakespeare Company, the National Theatre, the Donmar Warehouse and the Old Vic. They have discussed many projects that the public haven't seen, some of which have long since been abandoned or have arrived in other forms.

Fortunately, the tours have ensured that those productions that are not in the extensive archives of the National Theatre and the Royal Shakespeare Company have been captured at the Brooklyn Academy of Music and are now stored at the Lincoln Center Library for the Performing Arts in New York, where they can be viewed on video. It's an invaluable resource for charting the development of Sam and Simon's collaboration if you weren't in the original live audience. The media interest in their collaboration also provides a plethora of reviews that offer different perspectives on the development of their productions.

Naturally, this collaboration does not sit in isolation but is part of a larger network. There are several actors who have been involved in more than one of the productions discussed in this book – David Troughton, David Bradley, Cherry Morris, Paul Jesson and Selina Cadell for example – and there is the continued involvement of some of the same practitioners in the design teams. The work of Paul Pyant, as lighting designer for five of the plays, and Paul Arditti, as sound designer on four, has been an integral part of the developing process. Arguably the most prominent of these collaborators is Anthony Ward who has been the designer or set designer for every production with the exception of *Richard III*.

One of the unusual and idiosyncratic things about Sam and Simon's relationship is that it has developed solely through their continued collaboration; they rarely see each other outside of the bounds of a play. "The funny thing about our relationship is that outside of work we don't see very much of each other which is very strange," states Simon. "It's not deliberate. Sam has spent an increasing amount of time in America since 2003 so that's exacerbated it further. I'd love to see more of him and I enjoy his company. Occasionally there will be invites back and forth to birthday parties and obviously when his son was born I was in contact with him. In a way I love that. I think that it's rather *neat*. We're always talking about a project. We go off and do our separate things and then we meet every two years or so and do a show and, not to be sentimental about it, but we pick up exactly where we left off so it's not a strain."

Due to this 'neat' relationship, it's possible to explore what it means for a director and an actor to be involved in working together on eight or so productions across twenty years, without being affected by personal factors outside the rehearsal room. The contact that they have is conducted largely through and about projects and there are very few other creative partnerships that have lasted for as long that exist in the same way. Although they are clearly very good friends, and have a very special bond which is apparent when they talk about each other, this has developed through their collaboration and they have, in a sense, only known each other as director and actor.

"I'm very careful about using excessive words about Sam because when you really love somebody, as I do, and I love working with him, it's very easy to get all fluffy about the whole thing! I think Sam is unquestionably a very, very clever man. I don't say this out of false modesty but I don't think I am particularly clever. However, I am able to recognise cleverness in other people. He can wield an argument like nobody else actually, my God, can he really wield an argument. There are moments when you just think, 'Ah, yes, this is going to work.'"

"There were the very hard first shows: I didn't see his *Love's Labour's Lost* so I can't comment about that, but *Troilus and Cressida* and *Richard III*. They're hard, hard, black, black shows and they have a sort of adolescent mentality in a way so they're good for young men to do, especially *Richard III*. The emotional content is there but it's buried beneath the brittleness of the situation. Sam's intellect was very evident in *Richard III* and especially in *The Tempest*. Over the years that's changed slightly and he's become much more emotionally expressive in his shows; he has softened over the years. I started to notice a change happening around about *Othello*. I was very much still at the hard edge of that play but I think that Sam was more interested in the softer side, of love and things like that. And now, being a father, he's much more aware of the significance of children in the plays that we work on."

One of Sam's favourite phrases appears in the last few pages of Clive James' third volume of memoirs *May Week Was In June*. At the end of university, James wants to be a serious artist, but he has come to the realisation that he's not cut out to be a novelist, he's going to end up being a journalist.

"All I can do is turn a phrase until it catches the light."

"That's a great phrase because in writing that he's actually demonstrating what he's talking about: he's turning a phrase until it catches the light. Novalis' idea of 'making the familiar strange and the strange familiar' – turning something until it catches the light – is a lot to do with how you handle classical work, because there are so many things in it that are familiar and yet when you see them done well it's as if you've never seen it before."

"Simon's great art is that he can take a role and turn it until it catches the light. Sometimes he only turns it two degrees and bang. He's very, very clever in how he tells you to listen to something. If Simon decides that there is a line or a moment in the role that is the defining moment, the whole audience leaves knowing that it is the moment that he thinks sums up the entire play. He is not going to let that go. He will tell the whole audience, 'watch this...', this is the moment that makes sense of everything, and they'll all go away knowing it at exactly the same time. This is the centre of the performance and the play as written."

"Above all, what attracts both of us is that we are both very English in our love of irony and that sense of undercutting or subverting expectation," or in turning something and catching the light.

DISCLAIMER (!)

"You'll have to check all of this with Sam. My memory is very bad so this book will be entirely full of fabrications if we're not careful."

"My memory is slightly better than Simon's but I can't claim to it being brilliant. If there are 'Lies, Damn Lies, and Statistics,' then I think we're in the 'Damn Lies' section of proceedings."

CASTING

"I suspect that Sam thinks very long and hard about this"

As the director Sam has almost total control over the casting choice; Simon can only accept or decline a role. Even today, twenty years into their working relationship and with his status as a 'star actor', Simon must wait for Sam's telephone call. It's a perfectly normal arrangement and one that Simon feels is beneficial, given that he acknowledges that he has a terrible sense of his own casting.

"I'm very passive in this: I just wait for the phone call from Sam. I think it would be presumptuous of me to cast myself, because I can't see myself and, as has been frequently reported, I have a pretty bad self image. It's just something I don't think I do. If I suddenly had a passionate desire to do a part then I would feel that I was able to say something."

Simon Russell Beale is an unconventional leading man, predominately because of his physicality. Critics devote paragraphs of their reviews to his appearance and assess much of his performance based on his body shape. Added to this is Simon's self-criticism, which extends to his supposed inability to tackle accents or to adequately portray alpha males. For his first major interview, Simon had raced down from Newcastle to London still hung over and was in a more than usually self-critical mood. He told Paul Taylor of the Independent, "I hate my body, I hate my voice, so much of what I do on stage is saying 'Love me despite the fact that I'm ugly.'" It's a quote that he can still repeat verbatim today and accepts that, though the sentiment was exaggerated, there was a trace of truth in it.

Throughout his career at the RSC, Simon enjoyed a series of successes playing restoration fops, but was beginning to feel pigeonholed by these comedic turns. Through negotiation with the then Artistic Director Terry Hands, a package was created for Simon that would allow him to break through the stereotyping: Oswald in Ibsen's *Ghosts*, Konstantin in Chekhov's *The Seagull*, the title role in Marlowe's *Edward II* and, to begin with, Thersites in *Troilus and Cressida*, working with Sam for the first time.

Not that Simon's initial response to Thersites was wholly positive, indeed the first casting offer was an underwhelming experience: "I was at my parents' house in Tidworth. There was a phone call in the study room. It was Sam who said 'Would you like to play Thersites?' and I remember my heart sinking. I don't remember my bowels moving, as they do when I get offered a rather exciting part!"

That was because Simon was worried about being pigeonholed. "Clowns in Shakespeare are a nightmare and I'd already done the Shepherd in *The Winter's Tale* at the RSC. I didn't want to play another clown but I said yes because Sam was hot news. I thought: if he's asking then I better give it a whirl."

Prior to that phone call, Sam had already completed a directorial rescue mission on an ill-fated production of *London Assurance* at Chichester and managed to turn it into a success and at just twenty-four years of age, he had opened The Cherry Orchard in the West End starring Judi Dench. He was indeed 'hot news.'

"I'm not a very good caster of myself so if somebody thinks I can do something then I'd better trust that." In retrospect, the decision opened up a number of new doors for him. "Sam was a very important part of the process where an overweight actor who does comedy was allowed to do these much more serious roles. I'll always be grateful for that."

In the time between the casting offer and the first day of rehearsals, around any preliminary meeting, Sam will be assembling the full company. Between the offer of Thersites and the first day of work on *Troilus and Cressida* Sam assembled what he considers to be "probably even to this day, one of the best acting companies that I've ever put together and I still don't know how I did it. Ciaran Hinds, Norman Rodway, Amanda Root, Sally Dexter, in addition to Ralph [Fiennes] and Simon, David Troughton, Paterson Joseph: preposterously good really." The calibre of the acting is of course paramount, but the director must also keep in mind that he has to form a cohesive company. "I suspect that Sam thinks very long and hard about this; I think he takes great care at casting people that will get on together." Careful casting is essential when an ensemble are going to be in each other's company for an extensive period. The environment must be conducive to working within the blank space of rehearsals and continue being so through a lengthy performance run and potentially subsequent tours and transfers.

REHEARSALS

"Ensemble is not something that you can say you're going to create. Ensemble is the work."

As a young director Sam considered his approach in the first week of rehearsals to be "conventional". The actors would read through the play, there would be a discussion on the text and rehearsals would be conducted from the start of the play to the end. "We'll block Act I on Monday and Act II on Tuesday sort of thing. I was always keen to perfect a scene, or at the very least know that it could be correctly adjusted later, before I moved on so I would always take a long time staging."

"It's funny because running concurrent with my twenty years of working with Simon there has been the development of my own way of working which has also changed and, to a degree, that's changed because of my work with him. When I have a lead actor that I'm that relaxed with then I'm able to work in a very relaxed way. The way I work now is non-prescriptive and non-linear in the sense that I don't necessarily plough through the text from beginning to end working in detail. Now I don't worry about detail so much early on, I'm more interested in exploring all sorts of different alleyways within the process."

That has manifested itself in an approach where each character and scene is explored from a multitude of angles in an environment where nothing is 'right' or 'wrong.' Each scene is thoroughly workshopped, rarely repeating a particular set-up. Actors may be encouraged to play the scene sat at a table, then sat on the floor, then working closely together, then working at a distance, and so on. Sometimes actors will be asked to swap the characters they are playing in a scene.

"It's difficult to describe, but it's about understanding a scene through 360 degrees rather than through the prism of your own character. You understand the shape of it and the purpose of the character in the scene before you go into what's right or wrong: Do I sit? Do I stand? Do I pick something up here? Am I cleaning or am I pretending to clean? Am I looking at him or not looking at him? Am I communicating with him? Am I listening to what he's saying? Am I pretending to be nervous or am I really nervous? All of those things do have to be discussed." The discussion doesn't always occur in a quasi-classroom format about what was learned about any particular version of the scene, the discussion is implicit in the work. On occasion Sam will pull out something of interest, or ask an actor to reflect on what they've learnt about their character by playing the person interacting with them in a scene.

Eventually, shapes and threads within scenes may begin to develop. "The mystery with Sam," says Simon with a broad smile, "and he'll never let you know the truth, is whether it did occur through the process or whether he had it pre-planned." Sam will go so far as to say that he "may start a scene knowing a shape that I think is the right shape for it but I would never, ever say to the cast that's what it was until I absolutely have to because in the two days it takes me to explore that scene with them three or four better versions of it might emerge. The way I work is so without prescription now. That began with my production of *Othello*."

Simon concurs that "it was a pretty blank space in *Othello* but it did have defined areas and also a very definite time period and place. There was also the idea of film noir. Whereas when we started work on *Twelfth Night* it was an absolutely blank canvas. If I remember rightly I think *Twelfth Night* was when Sam started the idea of the circle and his desire that the full company should be there the whole time. It had been developing before, but there was an idea of us all sat around in the circle, on carpets, and everybody being there all of the time and not setting anything at all and having a totally blank space."

For *Twelfth Night* Sam had once again collected together a remarkable ensemble of actors: David Bradley, Paul Jesson, Helen McCrory, Cherry Morris, Mark Strong and Emily Watson amongst others. One can easily imagine the younger actors joining this company feeling a little daunted. "I suppose there is a sort of a responsibility – though that's too grand a word – there's a sense in which everyone should be aware of the dynamics going on and if it is daunting for other actors then you should make sure they're not daunted – though I don't know how you do that. Sam is fairly good at allowing everyone their say. In fact, he's got better and better at that I think. If somebody has something to say they're absolutely welcome to say it. One of the principle reasons for people to be there the whole time is to have lots of voices that are able to contribute otherwise, what's the point of them being there? I would hate to think that a long relationship like ours is in any way exclusive; that would be terrible."

Perhaps it's a measure of how inclusive the process is that even after twenty years of collaboration Simon still feels daunted on the first day of rehearsals. It's the process of the elaborate game playing that Sam constructs that generates the ensemble feel and binds a company together swiftly. "It is very nerve-wracking in the beginning even for me but it becomes a relaxing environment very quickly. Any nerves disappear quite quickly because what Sam gives the impression of doing is not really caring what you do particularly! It sounds utopian but nothing is right and nothing is wrong."

"Ensemble is not something that you can say you're going to create. Ensemble is the work," states Sam. "You have to work in a way that is basically democratic. You have to work in a way that allows for everybody's opinion and everyone's point of view and keep the channels open for as long as possible. At a certain point you have to say 'I'm the boss, this is how it's going to be.' If I don't make the decision nobody will. You can't say, 'I'm going to create an ensemble so let's all go for a company meal' or 'let's have a party.' That's just surface. Ensemble comes from mutual respect and mutual understanding and not only respect of what the actors are capable of but respect for their own space and their own processes."

Managing the various and varied needs of an ensemble can be a precarious balancing act for a director, particularly when actors' performances are developing at different speeds and at different stages within the process. If an actor wants to work quickly, the director has to accommodate that whilst also making sure that the other actors understand that they don't necessarily have to work at the same pace. "Some people will get freaked out and rush. They rush to make too many decisions. You can feel them try to paint the wall and blow the paint dry. And you have to say 'You only have to paint half of it today, you can paint the other half tomorrow and you can do the second coat next week. Then you can watch it dry slowly. You don't have to blow it and get the hairdryer out, just take your time. Just because Simon has got three coats on it and he's already drawing a mural on it doesn't mean that you have to!'"

Conversely, any actor that wants to work quickly must also be made aware that these other processes may involve exploring possibilities tangentially. "Sometimes I can feel Simon thinking 'Why are we wasting time on this, this is absolutely pointless, why are we debating this?' And I'm there to say 'No, we're allowed to do whatever is necessary at this moment.' I'll be the person to say when we don't have time for something, but in the early stages of rehearsal we have plenty of time. That's what we're here for. You have to let these things be explored. That's ensemble." It's a characteristic of the blank-canvas way of working that not only are ideas not immediately fixed, but that the process is fluid enough to encompass every actor's working methodology.

"Some of it is about pace and rhythm; some of it's just about psychology. Some people need encouragement and some people need challenge. Everybody needs to be told they're doing well at some point, but sometimes people need challenging and you need to say when they're not doing well enough. 'I know you can do better.' Sometimes you just need to be supportive. Everyone has a different language. Some of the best notes are delivered as a joke. You can change a whole performance in one line or you can destroy one if you deliver the wrong note at the wrong time. You can spend two hours giving notes and getting nowhere if you're not careful and you can spend two minutes and turn the performance on its head."

THEATRICAL GESTURES

"I'm just going to tell you my images"

It is highly likely that Sam and Simon are the first people into the rehearsal room every morning, as both like to arrive well in advance of the day of work beginning. They take this opportunity to have a five minute chat about what happened the day before. "I might say to Simon 'I thought it was very interesting when...,' but during the course of rehearsals, I'll be talking to him almost in semaphore, or whispering to him; I won't be stopping him from the doing of it."

Sam and Simon don't have lengthy, intellectual discussions about the work itself, certainly not during the process of rehearsing, but they instead communicate through what Sam calls "a lot of conversations in the cracks. It's much more to do with play. It's much more to do with finding three of four key images that have stimulated both of us simultaneously and working backwards from there."

That's not to suggest that their combined intellect, rigour and intelligence isn't at work within the rehearsal room. "You take it as fact that we've read the play properly and that we understand it and that we know the tradition of classical theatre in which we're working," states Sam.

Sam's intellectually informed practice can be seen in his approach to verse. At the beginning of rehearsals for *Othello*, for example, he took the company through the play from start to finish with a fine tooth comb "on the rather simple principle that if you can make the line fit a regular iambic pentameter stress then you should try it," remembers Simon. "If it really can't be iambic then it will have to be a trochee or a spondee or whatever although he never uses those words. I can remember that he was quite fussy actually, but then it's never really talked about again after that."

Instead, there is a process of "practical literary criticism"; the idea of understanding each element of every scene in a three-dimensional way. There are a series of small intellectual constructs – or "micro-arguments" as Simon refers to them – that are clarified and distilled into a line of thought, but these almost always take the actor into unexpected emotional rather than intellectual territory.

For this process, Simon attempts to rid himself of any preconceptions and assumptions and arrive "with the slate wiped clean". The reading process is therefore a live and active component of rehearsals and not just an academic exercise. It is what Simon calls "a theatrical Uncertainty Principle."

In addition, research does not form a large component of his preparation for any role. Of course the knowledge that Simon accumulates can inspire an image that stimulates him, but this is drawn from life experience and not from direct preparation for a role. "I didn't do any research on the historical Richard III for example, because there wasn't any point. He's obviously a much maligned man and I feel sorry for his memory, but the fact is that Shakespeare has written this quite immensely glamorous villain. He's endlessly fascinating and it really is the most brilliant exploration of what it is to be a dictator."

When approaching *Richard III* Simon hadn't even stopped to consider the theatrical lineage he was about to enter. "I remember just before we opened that there was an article that I saw by chance when I was reading the daily papers. It said 'The New *Richard III* at Stratford – Will he be as good as...?' and then there was a whole host of pictures of Olivier, Antony Sher, Ian Holm and that was the first time that it occurred to me that people would be looking at the production in that way. I got this terrible stomach ache, literally, I had a spasm. I had to go and have a hot bath. It never occurred to me that people would compare me to Ian Holm. He was the last person to play Richard III – at The Other Place, I think – so of course they were going to compare me to him. I never thought about it."

"I'm sure Sam was aware of it but it never occurred to me. It never crossed my mind that we'd only each done two of Shakespeare's plays previously and now we were going to tackle this Marlovian part: the arrogance of youth! I look back at some of the decisions I made and I think this is just absurd: I'd never do it now. But in a way *Richard III* is more direct and straightforward than *Troilus and Cressida*. If you can manage *Troilus and Cressida* you can probably manage to do a production of *Richard III*."

Simon had not seen either Ian McKellen or Antony Sher's performances and contemplated watching the Olivier film version but quickly switched it off thinking that "it wasn't wise to watch." He even joked with Sher about the memory of his 1984 performance. "He was actually next door rehearsing *Tamburlaine* while we were rehearsing. The wonderful thing about the part is that whatever you do it's going to be different. When I was first offered it I thought I would have to do something different with it to surprise people. But the way it developed was partly to do with Sam: he demanded very clear verse-speaking and he didn't want any tricks."

In his own efforts to read the role afresh and offer something new to this theatrical continuum, Sam was struck by a number of images. On the first day of rehearsals he shared them with Simon. "I said 'I'm just going to tell you my images: I think he should be a big man but he should just be on a tiny little bendy cane. I think we shouldn't see him to begin with; we should just hear him in the darkness...' I had images about his coronation, I thought we should see him fall and his inability to stand up. I had these images about the head of Hastings being in a cardboard box which came straight from the movie *Barton Fink*. There were a whole collection of these images. I'm sure there were images I had that I didn't use."

The only other actor with whom Sam has worked on this basis is Alan Cumming when they collaborated together on *Cabaret*. The role of the MC, originated by Joel Grey, is one that can change and adapt to fit the personality of any actor portraying him. "The MC is what you make of him really. Here are the eight images I have of him: I think he should bare his backside and he should have a swastika on his bum; we should project an image of Hitler over him so he stands in it; he sings along to a wind-up gramophone; he appears as a woman; he shape-shifts..." As with every production, not every visual idea appears in the finished article. "The Hitler image, for example, didn't go into that production, but what it did was to say to Alan, 'You can go anywhere with this, but here's these things that I think are interesting that I see when I'm reading the piece and listening to the music. Are any of them interesting to you?' And that worked very well with Alan."

It's also a process that works very well with Simon and has been a mark of their collaborations from their first production of *Troilus and Cressida*. "I had the image of Thersites with a jester's stick; there was a little hacker radio; or carrying a lunchbox around; or having a little table that he set his lunch out on. It's sort of pathetic: it had that lonely public-schoolboy/prep-schoolboy thing about it." It's a process that continues with the recent Bridge Project with Leontes in *The Winter's Tale*.

Simon was inspired by the figure of Phillip II of Spain. "He was ruling over the largest empire in the world, but was holed up in this great mausoleum palace of death outside Madrid where all of his ancestors were buried. He worked in a tiny little room with a desk, not delegating, doing all of the work for farmers' subsidies and whatever else they did in those days. It was just the minutiae of government and hours and hours and hours spent at a desk." This became a clue into the private life that Leontes may have been living in the passage of time when *The Winter's Tale* moves from Sicilia to Bohemia and returns again. "What does Leontes do for 16 years? He works. He just works to run the kingdom in a tiny study with no other occupation at all. That's all he's been doing for the sixteen years after Hermione's death: sitting in an office doing the paperwork."

The visual idea of "the lonely man working at his desk" is something that has an inexplicable resonance for Simon. "I have no idea where it comes from but I find it a very potent image. It's a single light sat on a desk and a man working overnight in front of it." It is an image that recurs with Iago in *Othello*, Leontes in *The Winter's Tale* and also for George in Tom Stoppard's *Jumpers* as directed by David Leveaux at the National Theatre and Philip in Christopher Hampton's *The Philanthropist* as directed by David Grindley at the Donmar Warehouse. "Yes! I'd never really thought about that. I can just see myself now saying 'Perhaps I need a desk in this one?!' Even doing a Houseman recital I did a couple of years ago at the National, I wanted it set up as a radio studio. I said I wanted a desk, a stand, a mic and a light and the rest should be absolutely blank. It was the lonely man working at his desk again. You've caught me out on one of my recurring leitmotifs!"

For Leontes, the image was explored extensively in rehearsals in a number of different formats, including one arrangement that Simon particularly enjoyed with the desk right at the foot of the stage with Leontes sat at work with his back to the audience. Eventually the idea was superseded by the image of Leontes and Paulina silently sitting together on a bench in the cemetery. "The really exciting response always comes from physicalising something; that's when something hits visually and I know what the impression is that Sam is trying to achieve. Paulina and Leontes sitting together were like Derby and Joan on a bench. 'There they sit, day by day / They do not talk, There is nothing to say.' They were just two old people united by this old grief."

The images aren't always predetermined and introduced on the first day of rehearsals or in a preliminary meeting. They can occur 'in the moment' in the midst of a scene being run or they can arrive gradually over the course of rehearsals as the thoughts generated by these micro-arguments begin to coalesce. "There's no set method for how ideas come out. Some you risk it is as you do it. Then there are others which require props which can be terribly impractical so therefore they have to be discussed beforehand as they require some stage management."

Sometimes, as the micro-arguments are distilled into a line of thought, the images arrive through a process of co-authorship. One of the images that were developing simultaneously in the minds of both the director and the actor was of Leontes and Mamillius consistently together. "I don't know when Sam had the idea of having Mamillius on stage so much throughout *The Winter's Tale* but there came a point when I remember saying 'I think he should be in on this scene,' and 'what if I wheel the boy on and tuck him back in his wheelchair and that covers that scene change.' I remember having that idea, which is a micro-idea, but it had been building in both of our heads. It's probably true of most things that they develop as a parallel thing."

This was combined with the sense of Leontes as another "lonely man working at his desk" and fed into an earlier study scene. It presented Leontes as an obsessive working man and that part of the reparation to his parenthood was that the boy would be in the study with him. "I liked the idea that he was abusing the child just by keeping his son with him the whole time."

Allowing an actor to introduce images and make these links is a major element of the blank-canvas way of working. There is an openness in allowing the actors to make their own connections. "Though you never know with Sam whether or not he had that idea long ago. He can be quite shrewd in keeping back information and releasing it at the right point which is a great directorial skill, allowing the actor to discover it, yet I remember that being an absolutely collaborative decision that Mamillus should be on stage with Leontes all the time."

Obviously, not all of the images that are investigated during the course of rehearsals are employed in the realised production. Sometimes through investigation better ideas will emerge and ideas are abandoned. Other times they are dismissed outright. "A conversation like that is easy with Sam. He just says 'No.' That very quickly turned into a habit with us that if he doesn't like something he just tells me so."

In a similar vein to his evocation of the figure of Phillip II for Leontes, Simon used a snippet of information about George VI for an image of the coronation scene in *Richard III*. Like the politicians of today, the monarch wore make-up for all of his public appearances. "So I decided that Richard would have to wear make-up but very badly. I might even have toyed with false eyelashes; I certainly had great big red cheeks. We must have tried that for a long time, at least long enough to make it to a Dress Rehearsal, because there's a photograph postcard of me in full-make up. Of course, I looked appalling, like a puppet or something. I think Sam probably thought I was going to do something more subtle." There is a running joke that exists between them about the tension between vulgarity and classicism and here there was a tension between the two and Sam cut the image.

"Sam is quite brutal with me sometimes, most of the time he just says 'no' but probably more often than I'm pretending he does say 'yes.' Most of the ideas for any of the productions for which they've become well known are in fact his and not mine! The big theatrical gestures are all his. Though, The Hilda Ogden moment was mine, actually. I'll claim to that!"

The 'Hilda Ogden moment' refers to a very particular event in the personal history of these productions. It arose initially from an intellectual construct regarding the significance of children. Throughout Shakespeare's career the relationship between parents and children and particularly the death of children has a profound impact on the shape of a play. Simon has noticed that Sam has become even more acutely aware of this thread in his own work since the birth of his own son, particularly with the Bridge Project productions.

Yet even during an early collaboration like *Richard III*, the importance of the deaths of the two young princes was developing mutually in the minds of both Sam and Simon. "It's these murders that are unforgivable. All of the other murders you think anybody else would have done them if they'd have had half the chance and half the wit that Richard has. Yet, the murder of the children, even the murderer Tyrell expresses his doubts. It's the turning point. I think Ian Richardson said that the turning point for Richard was the crowning but it's the same area of the play where the fun stops. The sheer horror of those deaths was a mutual thing for Sam and me."

In searching for an image that encapsulated this intellectual construct, Simon sought inspiration from an unlikely source. In November 1984, ITV screened an episode of *Coronation Street* in which long-serving character Stan Ogden died. His devoted wife Hilda looked through his possessions from the hospital during the end credits, which for the first time were played without the signature theme tune. "I don't remember whether I'd seen it years before or if it had been repeated on television recently but there was that very famous ending with no music where Hilda opened Stan's effects from the hospital. It was loaded with significance."

Simon decided that when Tyrrel returned having completed the murders of the princes, he should return with their pyjamas. On this occasion the image needed to be discussed and planned in advance because it involved the use of a prop. When Tyrell handed Richard the pyjamas, Richard sniffed them. "I wanted to smell the talc," says Simon. "It was another battle of vulgarity versus taste and that was a borderline one for Sam." It was a visual idea that remained in the final production.

"It's a strength I don't have but Sam has a very good eye and very clear style. It became a very dominant style at the Donmar about how you do great classical plays: very clear, very symmetrical, his critics would claim 'antiseptic' but it's very beautiful to look at. It's ravishing. You can see that right the way through to *The Winter's Tale*. He loves his candles! I have a slightly dirtier take, but then I'm not responsible for the whole design."

This 'dirtier take' manifests itself in a variety of sensory approaches for Simon. The characters he plays make a great deal of contact with chairs, tables and the rest of the physical environment that they inhabit. Being this tactile is a useful way of grounding a character in a space. "I do have a tendency to want to pick my nose or to spit or to... it's bodily fluids actually."

"That's the interesting thing about physicality. People think that rehearsing is all about the brain, and I do tend to work an argument through, but unquestionably the exciting moments are when it becomes a physical expression of something. I'm probably more physical than people think."

'THE JUMP'

"It has to cost you something"

Over the course of the rehearsal period, the images are introduced, investigated and decided upon to create the broad emotional landscape of the character. Slowly, as the actor follows the character's journey, the details are fed in and linked and the performance starts to cohere. The director refines an actor's performance by giving him precise notes. Crucially, for the note to be most effective, the way it is delivered is almost as important as the note itself.

There is a book about the first production of *The Heiress* on Broadway called *Watchman, What of the Night?* by Jed Harris. In the appendix to the book a stage manager from the original version of Thornton Wilder's *Our Town*, which Harris also directed, offers a story about the director which has become one of Sam's favourite anecdotes about how a simple directorial note can transform an actor's performance. Thorton Wilder was watching a run-through and thought that the actor playing the Stage Manager – a character in the play who directly addresses the audience – was ruining the production by sentimentalising the role. Wilder approached Harris instructing him to fire the actor and Harris said that he would deal with it.

The stage manager writing the appendix reports that Harris initiated another run-through informing the company that the previous one was great and that they were going to do it again. Wilder was apoplectic because he didn't want to watch that actor's terrible performance as the Stage Manager all over again. In between the run-throughs, Harris walked up onto the stage and spoke to the actor. Harris delivered a brief note to the actor and they both laughed. Harris returned to his seat, the run-through resumed and the actor gave an entirely different performance. Following that rehearsal, Wilder approached Harris to find out what he had said. Harris responded "All I said was, 'a little less cello.' That's all I said."

"It's a wonderful book and that's a great story", says Sam. "Sometimes that kind of note placed right can just unlock somebody. Someone will understand that note. To the right actor at the right time that's a brilliant note." It follows, of course, that this type of note is not suitable for every kind of actor. "Some actors wouldn't know what you were talking about because they wouldn't think of themselves as a musical instrument and couldn't deal with a note in those terms."

An understanding of how each actor in the company works is vital to any director in order to be able to articulate a note in terms that the actor will comprehend. "There are visceral actors and there are musical actors. There are emotional actors and there are intellectual actors. To an actor like Helen McCrory, for example, I could say 'You should play the second act like you're having your head held under water,' and she would absolutely get the sense of that, but she wouldn't know what I was talking about if I mentioned a cello. 'Having your head held under water' would be meaningless to Simon yet I could say to him 'a little less cello,' and he'd get it straight away."

Sam would use that sort of note once the general form and the emotional landscape of the performance is in place. "If you'd describe the cello note as a technical note, then the majority of notes that I'd give him would be technical or tone notes rather than psychological notes because Simon doesn't miss the core of the character." If the core of the character isn't in place, then an actor's performance can drift, particularly over the course of a long run or a world tour. "I came back to my first production in New York of *Cabaret* after about six months. There was a brilliant actor who had literally forgotten the character he was playing. I told him that everything that you're doing looks good and sounds good but has absolutely nothing to do with the character you were originally playing. Sometimes you have to be challenging. It's about cutting your suit according to your cloth as far as dealing with every actor. Everyone needs something different."

One of Sam's major passions is cricket and, at one time, being a cricketer was a serious alternate career path for him. Simon draws parallels between Sam's skills as a director and those he would use as the captain of a cricket team. "The idea of a psychological understanding of all of his players is something that he certainly carries over into the rehearsal room."

This man-management is also evident in the way Sam changes his approach to meet the needs of each actor on an individual basis. "I'll always remember him talking to me about solus calls which made me laugh a lot." Solus calls are one-on-one sessions scheduled throughout rehearsals between a director and each of the principal actors. "He said 'One actor comes in and works hard for a full hour. Another actor comes in with a very big idea that you spend the whole hour trying to change.'" And Simon? "He said, 'You come in and work very, very, very hard for twenty minutes and then you just want to gossip. Everyone has a different requirement. I recognise that that is what is needed.' He's always been very acutely aware of his skill there."

It is possible that over the course of rehearsals, and certainly across twenty years of collaboration, an innate understanding of how each individual operates can develop. "I know that I don't often let Sam complete a sentence in rehearsal. He'll start to talk about something and then I'll say, 'Yeah, I've got that, I know where we're going with that,' and Sam would acknowledge that as well. It's interesting because you can see with a colleague of this long how ideas develop. I think that it's unquestionably true that we have a shorthand. I can't quite put it into words; I don't know when the shorthand applies."

Understanding how that actor works can also lead to an ability to identify the times when an actor can take being pushed further and when they need support. "For the most part Sam's actually quite good at stroking me at the right time. In Madrid on *The Winter's Tale* I had a sudden loss of self confidence which happens every so often on stage, particularly on a world tour when you're tired. On this occasion he said 'You just need a hug, don't you?' It just made me think 'Okay, he still believes in me so that's fine.' He's very good at man-management."

Perhaps the most constructive word to describe any good directing is *balance*. Being able to negotiate the fine line between the emotional and the intellectual, between the visceral and the musical, between classicism and vulgarity and between reassurance and challenge is the hallmark of any good director. To be able to do this on a case by case basis with each individual member of a company and to create an environment that is open enough to accommodate each actor's processes and opinion is surely the hallmark of a great director. The rehearsal room, then, is a complex arena of negotiations and managing that room is a massive responsibility.

Inevitably, mistakes can be made. "I remember directing Alison Steadman and I'm sure that for about two months she thought I was absolutely useless because on the first day I gave her a note way too big to be appropriate for that stage of the rehearsals and it took me a long time to win her trust back. It was the wrong note at the wrong time. That's how you learn as a young director: you make some mistakes. You've got to admit when you're wrong."

Having worked extensively in both theatre and film, Sam is aware that the specific medium informs the negotiation of the actor-director relationship. "In films it's more obvious because people are divided up much more. With a company on stage you're not as able to isolate people and talk to them individually. On a film set you can always pick off an actor and go into a corner and have a quick word or whisper in their ear before the camera rolls, or even when the camera's rolling if it's a close-up. It's much easier to have a dialogue."

In the theatre, particularly when the rehearsals are structured around everyone being present all of the time, it's obviously much more complicated. Even when the nerve-wracking initial rehearsals are over and a level of trust has been established, the rehearsal room can be very exposing. There needs to be an atmosphere where actors are entitled to fail, otherwise they will not be encouraged to make more daring choices. Any constructive criticism must therefore be well timed and appropriately handled.

"Sometimes there's a time to expose someone in a company notes session if you're being really tough with them and sometimes you need to make it private. Sometimes there's a good time to do something that everyone knows about. For example, if everyone is aware that someone is giving a performance that's just a little bit over the top sometimes it's good, if it's the right actor and you know that they can take it, to make a joke out of it in a notes session. They'll laugh and the cast will laugh and they'll be aware that in the cast laughing, everyone agrees with the note."

Simon isn't exempt from being exposed to criticism within the company. In some ways, he's more susceptible, as Sam is quickly able to identify when Simon is resorting to a gimmick or safe mode that he's used many times before. "I can't really tell you what the tricks are because I don't know what they are but I know that whenever he comes to see me in a performance I always have a voice running in the back of my head. I'm sure this happens to a lot of actors: you're giving the performance and simultaneously you're thinking 'Oh, he'll like this, but he really won't like this. He wouldn't have allowed me to have done this.' Occasionally, you'll get him laughing by himself at one little bit, because he recognises some terrible old trick that's suddenly reappeared. That's always very gratifying!"

Ultimately, the approach will be dependent on the actor, the note and the stage of rehearsals. "There are a thousand ways of talking to any actor in a given moment. It all depends on who they are. It's purely instinctive on the part of the director: I can feel that now is the time to say this. You have to pick your moments with absolute care," and even then, the note may not have an immediate effect and compromises may need to be made. "I do have disagreements with Sam. There are things that he wants and I feel are wrong and I'll try. There have been things that I wouldn't have kept but I did keep because Sam wanted it."

Sam is continually pushing Simon to try harder and to go further in every aspect of his performance. Eventually one comes to a point in rehearsal when the images are in place and the emotional landscape of the character has become more coherent and the actor needs to move to the next level of performance. "You build up a lot of information and you build up a lot of decisions and you build up a lot of repressed emotional energy. Then all of these elements require that moment when you have to 'jump.'"

"There's always a point in rehearsal, especially with the hugely emotional roles when the jump has to be made and I'm well aware that Sam prepares me for that. He is very good at pushing me until the moment where I pop. The timing is not conscious on my part. I suspect, being the machiavel that he is, it may be conscious on Sam's, as it is with a lot of directors. They read a moment when you're going to make the jump. I remember precisely when it was with Uncle Vanya and with Leontes. I know exactly the day."

This can be one of those moments of challenge and Sam admits that sometimes as a director you have to be a bully. "I'd say to Simon 'Come on, you know what you've got to do, now do it. You've got to do it.' 'Really – do I really have to do it?' 'Yes, you have to go there.' It has to cost you something. You can't get away with it, you can't skirt around it. You can't find other ways of expressing it; it's just raw emotion and you have to find a way of dredging it up every night. I'm not going to interfere with where you get it from or where you find it. I'm not an acting teacher; I don't talk about sense memory and all of that stuff. I'm not in the business of telling you how to achieve an emotional pitch but you have to achieve that."

Simon's resistance to the moment where you have to jump is because he is "reticent about being emotionally vulgar. I'm wary of the big outpouring. It was the same with the fury at the end of *The Life of Galileo*, a National Theatre production directed by Howard Davies. I know Sam is aware of this and I'm well aware that he's waiting."

A comparison of the dynamics of Vanya and Leontes is interesting. Both of them have difficulty sleeping and both begin their respective journeys on a very high pitch. "You could say that they're both roles that need someone who is willing to dive in, to step into the cold shower in an instant," says Sam. "Iago does not start the play with his plan fully formed. Malvolio starts in the background in his first scene. And I think that, on the whole, that's how Simon likes it to be. I think any actor does. Please don't make me come on and have to grab the bull by the horns straight away. Some parts just demand that."

In the end, making the jump becomes inevitable. "He needed a bit of pushing but I know him very well and I can look at him and say 'In your heart you know what you have to do and you have do it. There's nothing else that I can say. Everything else is in place. You know what the part is. You know who he is. You know the landscape of this person intimately now. You have to commit emotionally.'"

TECH, DRESS, PREVIEWS AND PRESS

"Sorry it's not working, we're scrapping it completely"

In *National Service*, his diaries of his tenure as Director of the National Theatre, Richard Eyre writes for his entry on 16th February 1989 "Talk to Mark Henderson (Lighting Designer) after the run-through... It's there, he says. What are you going to do now? Two weeks to go and I feel that it's a good piece of work – if I can translate it from the rehearsal room to the stage. It's like carrying water in your hands."

He is writing about his production of *Hamlet* with Daniel Day Lewis, but he could just as easily be referring to any production in any venue at any time. Even in theatre's subsidised sector, in great institutions like the National Theatre where rehearsal rooms are the same dimensions as the stages they adjoin, the transition from the rehearsal room to the stage can be a daunting prospect as productions can change immeasurably when they are put inside a set. The great discoveries of the rehearsal room can easily slip through your fingers.

"If you're lucky then there isn't an enormous leap from the atmosphere of the rehearsal room to the atmosphere of the stage," says Sam. "That's if you're lucky! Sometimes you can find that what you have in the rehearsal rooms is dwarfed by scenic ideas." Given the lengths to which Sam and his design team go to create as blank a canvas as possible for the ideas of the text, it is unsurprising that there haven't been any major design errors that he and Simon have had to overcome during their collaborations.

Even so, the technical rehearsal is still the first opportunity that the actors have to enter the fully realised world of the play for the first time. "It's a time when they need to feel out the actual physical environment. You need to give them space to do that. I feel that I have to stay in touch with the actors but I try not to load them down with too much new information and treat it as just another stage of the rehearsal process rather than a barrier."

They can often be a lengthy process that requires a great deal of stamina and patience from all concerned as sections of the production are tried, revisited, re-plotted and retried and each technical element is not without its complications. For his part, Simon is very self-contained during these periods. "He's an inordinately dependable man. There is a steely core there. He plays the role of 'Oh, I'm just a big, old, soppy actor,' but you only need to listen to his lecture on Shakespeare, or work with him, or discuss thorny points with him to know that he is as tough as nails. Don't be fooled. I don't mean tough in an unpleasant way. I mean that he knows what he thinks."

One of the things which allow Simon to explore the physical world comfortably is that, in his process of working from the inside out, the character's interior landscape has been fully realised. "Often the core of Simon's performance will be unchanged from very early on in rehearsals. He latches on to two or three central things and explores them fully. He doesn't slide around and throw in big, new things in previews. He's not made that way."

Part of Simon's resilience throughout the technical period is having the ability to laugh and enjoy the process. "At the end of the day we do make jokes to one another because there are some things that really make him laugh, which is always very pleasing, of course."

One of their many running jokes arose from the technical rehearsals for *The Tempest*. "When I was doing Ariel in this long tech and I was bored and I was just in my bare feet, I started doing contemporary dance for him." It's an amusing way of passing time during technicals that has continued throughout their career. "I was doing contemporary dance throughout the tech of *Uncle Vanya.* If you're hanging around because the technical team are addressing the lights or whatever, just do contemporary dance. It makes Sam laugh a lot."

Adding the technical dimension inevitably changes not just Simon's performance, but the production as a whole and this process of evolution continues throughout the previews. "I do an enormous amount of work in previews in particular. I can honestly say that I can re-rehearse the whole play during the course of the preview period." Having recently been through the process with his latest production of *As You Like It*, the first show in the second phase of The Bridge Project in New York, Sam estimates that 60% of the scenes had major changes in them and 40% of the scenes had minor changes but that nothing was left untouched.

Previews are often the point at which Sam pushes Simon the hardest. "Because I know what he's capable of, I'm less willing to accept a performance from him that would be a very good performance for some other people. Another director may be in awe of him at these times but they wouldn't know him as well. I use different criteria on Simon, I'm always pushing hard on everyone during previews and I know that Simon can take it. I know him so well I am tougher on him." Simon might be forgiven for thinking that on occasion there must be other actors that would need pushing just as hard as he does. Sam would counter that "I wouldn't be talking to them; I'd be talking to him. It's not a competition. I want everyone to be the best that they can be."

That was certainly the case for both *Uncle Vanya* and *The Winter's Tale* when, on both occasions, Sam was pushing Simon to be more daring right from the top of the play and to do more preparatory work before he walked on stage to initiate the right emotional state. "I felt that he was coasting during those early previews. Vanya and Leontes are both characters that have to bring their crises on with them very early on in the play. The play won't support you; you have to make a decision. Vanya when he walks on stage is already in the throes of desperate love with Yelena; is already hating Serebryakov; is already boiling in his own skin; is already in crisis before the play even starts. Similarly, Leontes has to leap immediately into the throes of jealousy which presumably has to have in some way predated the action of the play. The flaw has to be present in him long before the event of his jealousy."

This intense period of challenge can give rise to disagreements. "We had a couple of feisty previews [in *Uncle Vanya*] and on *The Winter's Tale* we had an occasional minor spat. I was pushing him to be more committed to a very specific, very detailed set of emotions. I told him he wasn't allowing the jealousy to take hold of Leontes. I felt he was in control of his jealousy, rather than letting the jealousy control him. He got upset because he thought he was doing well, which of course he was."

"He stomped off and I called him in his apartment about an hour later. He said 'Thanks for calling, I'm fine now' and that was it. I wanted him to know that I knew how brilliant he was being and I told him that he was amazing. 'I'm only pushing you because I know that you can do better; you're better than this so don't get cross with me for pushing.' He said 'I know and I love you for that but I also hate you sometimes too!' That sometimes seems to be the relationship between an actor and a director, or a player and a coach, or whatever you want to say."

"At some point, every actor needs unadulterated praise, and Simon is no exception, but what he often gets is me saying that it was okay but that he could do better! It can leave him temporarily frustrated, but previews *are* for pushing."

Throughout the work in previews, images and ideas can still be rejected and superseded. "One thing that is an absolute hallmark of Sam's is that he has no pride about jettisoning what seem to be good ideas." During *Troilus and Cressida*, the group of actors playing the warriors had spent an hour every morning of the full course of rehearsals, learning a choreographed sequence that emulated the routines of spinning guns from regiments of America and Canada. "They spent hours developing this routine – thank goodness not involving me – where they spun these sticks. It was a lot of work. It got right up to the wire on that one and Sam just said 'Sorry, it's not working, we're scrapping it completely."

"He said it absolutely clearly. He's very good at those very firm decisions where he admits that it was wrong. As it happened the lads were rather pissed off because they'd spent so many hours developing this routine and it was looking good. That wasn't the point: Sam knew it was structurally wrong. He's always been like that." As it happened, Sam believed that the best way to begin the production was the way that Shakespeare had written it: a prologue followed by the very intimate scene between Cressida and Pandarus.

It's a quality that Sam can also identify in Simon. "I think, like me, he's also very quick to try an idea out without any concern. Quick, quick, go, he has such facility that he can do it. It won't throw him to do it in the middle of a performance. He's also quite quick to admit when it doesn't work which I am too. I think that being confident and being right and being confident and being wrong is something we're quite similar about so our rhythms are quite similar. He doesn't agonise over things and neither do I. He's quite happy to work 'from the outside in.' He'll take a crazy idea and try it without any shame."

The previews are also the first time that the production has engaged directly with an audience. The audience response can immeasurably alter the dynamic of any scene that is put in front of them. Often each audience has an individual response and it is this element that can lead performances to change on a nightly basis. Each audience dictates its own particular rhythm and the story becomes clearer when it is in front of an audience by virtue of the production becoming storytelling. "Things that you were happy with suddenly seem leaden and things that you were worried about take off and the audience love them. After the first preview, there's a lot of work to do, you are always responding very quickly."

As part of the balance and tension between the two of them, Sam isn't just challenging Simon but Simon is pushing Sam too. "He does push me to be better. I learn a lot from him." During the first preview of *The Winter's Tale* in New York, the audience were laughing at Leontes at the beginning of the play. "I thought that it was terrible that they weren't taking him seriously. I went around to the dressing rooms afterwards and Simon was delighted:

> 'Did you hear how much they laughed?' he said.
> 'Yes, how do you feel about that?'
> 'I'm thrilled.'
> 'That's interesting, why?'
> 'They're with me at the beginning and they're engaged and then gradually what was once funny, almost absurd, becomes progressively more serious. If they're with me in the start in that way then I can turn them.'"

It's another example of Simon turning something until it catches the light. On this occasion, he is once again subverting the audience's expectation and response. "He was absolutely delighted with the laughter and then he controlled it successfully. He didn't stop it, he never wanted to stop it, but he didn't let it get out of hand to the point at which it became silly. He was sure that they were with him, that they were listening and that they knew what part of the journey we were on. He thought 'Sure, they're not taking Leontes' jealousy seriously here but in two scenes time they will and by the end of the play they certainly will be.' So, the laughter was just the beginning of Leontes journey and the audience's response to him. "He taught me so much about audience engagement. Laughter is not always bad in a tragedy nor is seriousness in a comedy."

In terms of learning about one another, it was during the preview period for *Troilus and Cressida* that the level of man-management that Sam undertakes during every production became crystal clear to

Simon. Simon's digs were directly opposite the stage door and Sam stayed there with him during the previews. "Watching him during that period was very interesting. He used to come back with a notepad filled with notes he'd obviously called to the assistant director. You know 'Simon – shit, Ralph – crap,' or whatever. He transformed these notes into beautifully, psychologically delicate encouragements. He's always been very good on that. In fact, he probably prides himself on that."

Even with the right amount of technical and man-management, every production is susceptible to technical difficulties. During the first preview of *Twelfth Night* in New York, when David Bradley (Andrew Aguecheek) and Paul Jesson (Toby Belch) contorted their bodies to accompany the fart sound effects during the catch scene, the speaker broke and no noise came out. "There was only one person laughing at that point in the auditorium and that was me!", says Sam. "They'd twisted their bodies as if to let rip an enormous fart and nothing happened and the audience didn't know what they were doing. That absolutely killed me."

"As long as they're not life-threatening, I laugh a lot when people make mistakes. I find the whole thing very funny. Theatre is absurd. You're only ever a slight mistake away from complete mayhem. The fact that people get through to such a degree is amazing. It's my childish sense of humour."

Of course, when a simple mistake is made at a vital moment, the other response is outright anger. During the Press Night for *The Winter's Tale* in London, there was an operator error and the lights didn't come up for the pivotal final scene of reconciliation. "The audience must have thought that was a daring thing for Mendes to do: not turn the lights on for the whole scene. They must keep the statue of Hermione in a dark room somewhere!" This was certainly not a laughing matter. "It was terrible. Simon was absolutely incandescent – which I've rarely seen him – he was furious and rightly so. It couldn't have been a worse moment to go wrong."

Press Nights are incredibly peculiar occasions. Arriving at the end of the preview period they are a sort of 'all or nothing' event as the production is unveiled to the critics. The auditorium is filled with reviewers, friends of the cast and creative team, and complimentary ticket holders if required to ensure a full house. "It's an insanely false dynamic," says Sam. "I much prefer the American system where the press are spread out across several performances. The actors don't know when each of them is in."

"The history of British Theatre is actually not the history of British Theatre; it's the history of Press Nights," he continues. "Critics are only ever reporting what the first night is like. Nobody seems to care after that. We're a bit trained at the moment into a process of announcing a play, rehearsing quickly, opening the show, it's either a hit or a flop, then it closes and you leave. The work there is very localised and it doesn't grow, change or morph."

Just as plays transform when they transfer from the rehearsal room to the technical world and scenes are altered and adjusted throughout the preview process, productions too develop and alter through the run of performances.

"One of the things that I love about The Bridge Project is that what arrives at the Old Vic is quite different from what has played at Brooklyn, Madrid, Amsterdam and Paris. What arrives at Epidaurus following the run at the Old Vic will be different again. That's the pleasure of it. The Bridge forces you into constantly reconsidering and re-evaluating what you've done. It's not a case of what is better or what is worse. It's just different. It changes."

Just as the engagement with an audience can alter the way a production is perceived, so the dimensions, acoustics and layout of a venue can affect how the show is received. Different aspects of the production come to the fore in more intimate houses; different things come to the fore in an amphitheatre when you're observing the production looking down onto the occasion rather than up to the stage. "It's a quite different sense of the play and a different sense of the performance and what the actors are trying to achieve even if the performances that they're giving are largely similar."

On the Press Nights themselves Simon is remarkably consistent. "He gets nervous, but not excessively so, he just gets on and does it. When he's doing it he's almost always 'in the zone' as they say in sports." Sam, on the other hand, can barely stay in the building, and certainly not in a seat in the auditorium. He may listen to proceedings backstage over the tannoy or leave the building for a drink and return to watch the final scenes from the back of the auditorium. "I'm an inveterate wanderer during those times. I rarely watch. I can't sit in my seat. I tend to make myself scarce. I find them unbearably tense."

Glancing through the reviews of these productions it seems a rare occurrence that Sam needs to be particularly worried. Even the early features of *Troilus and Cressida* were singing his praises. A magazine article in the *Observer* featured "Caroline Loncq (friend of Sam's at Cambridge and RSC actress) say[ing] 'He's not dogmatic. He's good at editing and manipulating. He works in pictures. He is good at hooking on to an emotional picture; he has a sense of its colour. He always knows what effect he wants to achieve.' The first thing Sam does is ask (like the teacher that he briefly was)

'Why are we performing this play?'"

A LONG RUN AND TOURING

"Look after yourself; it's a ball breaker"

Even when a production is robustly built, the experience of a lengthy international tour can still take its toll on the cast. The architecture of every auditorium can affect the relationship between the performer and the audience. Each stage and auditorium can vary in size, shape, acoustics and distance from the audience, which can affect the blocking of the show, the vocal quality of the performer or the scale of their performance.

In comparison to the cavernous space of the Wellington Opera House on the international tour of *Othello*, the Donmar Warehouse, one of the venues on the national tour of *Richard III*, can definitely be described as intimate. This can change the dynamic of the performance. When addressing soliloquies to the audience, for example, it is impossible to offer a general blanket cover, with the actors' eye contact drifting across the dark void of the auditorium. There the audience members are very present and very palpable – the actors and the audience occupy the same space – and they must be directly engaged in the soliloquy. At this stage, Simon had little experience of performing in the space. "My knowledge of the Donmar was very limited having only done two performances there."

Just as every venue has its own idiosyncrasies, so each new audience brings with it a new dynamic. Even a production that has a limited engagement in a single theatre can be altered on a nightly basis by the dynamic of the audience watching it. Like Sam, who will re-rehearse scenes during previews because of the altered dynamic now that the show is being seen by an audience and not in the vacuum of a rehearsal room, Simon is acutely aware of an audience; he can feel what a particular audience wants on a particular evening and will recalibrate his performance accordingly.

On an international tour, of course, there is the added dimension of performing to audiences for whom English is not their native language.

This can have a detrimental effect on the subtlety of the acting and lead to a danger of actors 'signposting' what is going on within the narrative arc in order to ensure that the audience understands what is taking place. Simon acknowledges that this was certainly the case for *Othello.* "We'd done something like three weeks in Tokyo, two weeks in Korea, a week in Beijing, Shanghai and Hong Kong so quite a long time with quite a lot of performances for non-English speaking audiences. That can tempt you into a different type of acting. I think that we had become portent."

If actors do fall into the habit of signposting this can usually still be corrected by a director, even if the production is on tour. Throughout the course of any run, a director will return to see a performance periodically, in order to provide notes to the actors. Sometimes this is conducted by an assistant, associate or staff director. Generally this is a caretaking capacity to maintain a consistent quality for the production but can be used as a means of re-invigorating a tired company, or provoking new thoughts to the actor that offer fresh motivation for the character.

Sam believes very much in the old theatrical joke about a director returning to a show halfway through a run and removing all of the actors' 'improvements'. "That's basically what I do with Simon! Having said that, he's amazingly consistent in a run; you can't really fault him in that. It's an astonishing thing. The general issue during a run is the lack of forward momentum. With most actors, they can sometimes fall in love with moments and forget the overall shape of the story."

Even when the production visits a country for which English is also the first language, cultural differences will lead an audience to receive a production differently. For Sam, *Othello* is not a play about race so much as it is about sexual jealousy. However, in America, with its acknowledged and self-evident race relations issues, "the language is the same but the attitudes are different."

Following the dates in Japan, Korea, Hong Kong and China, which had led to slightly portentous acting, the production arrived in New Zealand. "We'd just done a very, very long tour, it was very tiring and we got very bad reviews in New Zealand. It wasn't entirely our fault; we were in the wrong theatre," suggests Simon, demonstrating how the size of an auditorium can have a detrimental effect. "This is not an excuse, but we were put in the Opera House in Wellington which is very, very large. This was a production that started in the Cottesloe, the smallest of the National Theatre's three auditoria. It was partly our fault; we'd obviously become tired and lost something."

The acting company became very worried by the reviews because the next stop on the tour was at the Brooklyn Academy of Music in New York. "We panicked and we phoned Sam and asked him to come to Australia (which was our next visit) urgently! Really urgently!" At that time Sam was putting his new version of *Cabaret*, which had originated at the Donmar Warehouse, onto Broadway. "He obviously got this message in New York and thought 'I can't fly to Australia to see a show!'"

Sam was sent a video of the show and having watched it returned a series of comments, many of which were not directly referring to an actors' performance. Every single actor received a simple question. It's a technique that he'd later adopt during *The Cherry Orchard*, only on that occasion it was framed as 'Things I want to believe.'

"I've never heard of a director doing this and it was the first time he'd used the technique when I'd worked with him. It was actually rather magical. My favourite one was Montano which is a very small role and who is the Governor of Cyprus. The question was 'Does Montano enjoy his job? I remember thinking: that's brilliant."

The question that Simon received was 'When does Iago have his first drink of the day?' "The early drinking one was great. Iago did drink on stage certainly but we hadn't discussed whether or not he might be an alcoholic. They were all questions that had almost been talked about but not quite and so the comments Sam sent through just tipped you over and that's fantastic. That's a significant help. That was just to give a tired company a little bit of extra impetus."

Tours require a great degree of stamina and, particularly when undertaking large scale classical work with a degree of physicality, they can be physically as well as emotionally demanding. Simon didn't pay attention to his health during the run and subsequent tour of *Richard III* and paid the price for it. "He did what all Richard the Thirds have done since time immemorial and he did his back in because he was walking entirely on one leg; all the usual stuff. He overworks of course and takes a lot on. I wouldn't say too much as he's capable of doing it, but he does push himself too hard." Simon remembers the experience with dread. "It was an awful, awful time. Sam did say to me at the beginning: 'It's a ballbreaker, look after yourself.' And I didn't."

Simon had slipped his disc and although it was possible to work through the pain to a point it soon became clear that he couldn't return to the show. The doctor informed him that he needed an operation followed by a minimum of one month's rest. "There was one night when he was literally ashen on stage, I didn't think he was going to get through the show. In the fight at the end with Richmond, which was supposed to be a big sword fight, he just threw himself on the ground and presented himself for Richmond to kill. It was like self-sacrifice because he literally couldn't pick up the sword."

Sam spent three days rehearsing Ciaran Hinds into the role to take over from Simon. The turnaround was so swift that all of the front-of-house photos and publicity material still read 'featuring Simon Russell Beale.' "The audience were coming to watch Ciaran that night and we were literally slipping the programmes and then this self-pitying figure appeared in the lobby of the Donmar, just standing there and looking forlorn."

It was Simon who, two days after the operation, had felt a pang of neglecting the production. "I said 'Don't stand in the lobby of the theatre. What are you doing here?!' He said 'What do you mean? I just felt that I needed to be here to say sorry and to support people.' It then became clear to me that he'd had a couple of pints too many and was feeling a bit maudlin."

"I said 'Get out of the theatre! Get out!' I literally threw him out of the lobby and he stomped off down Earlham Street towards Seven Dials. I felt terrible afterwards for this poor guy so I trotted after him and apologised. I didn't mean to be rude but people were being told that he wasn't on that night and there he was standing in the lobby. That was the time when I had to be toughest with him because he'd slipped his disc and I had to ban him from the theatre!"

Simon will always remember the incident for its positive connotations: "That was the best show of *Richard III* I ever did when I couldn't move. Isn't that a great lesson for an actor? A lesson in economy and anger."

TROILUS AND CRESSIDA

"Thersites was like putting together a Frankenstein's monster"

TROILUS AND CRESSIDA by WILLIAM SHAKESPEARE
FIRST PERFORMANCE: Swan Theatre, Stratford-Upon-Avon, 18 April 1990

CAST

SIMON RUSSELL BEALE	Thersites
SIMON AUSTIN	Antenor
RICHARD AVERY	Calchas
MICHAEL BOTT	Helenus
ALFRED BURKE	Nestor
SALLY DEXTER	Helen
MIKE DOWLING	Aeneas
RALPH FIENNES	Troilus
MICHAEL GARDINER	Menelaus
SHURA GREENBERG	Paris' servant
CIARAN HINDS	Achilles
PATERSON JOSEPH	Patroclus
SYLVESTER MORAND	Agamemnon
RICHARD RIDINGS	Ajax
NORMAN RODWAY	Pandarus
AMANDA ROOT	Cressida
JULIE SAUNDERS	Andromache
LINDA KERR SCOTT	Cassandra
GRANT THATCHER	Diomedes
DAVID TROUGHTON	Hector
JOHN WARNABY	Paris

CREATIVE TEAM

SAM MENDES	Director
ANTHONY WARD	Designer
GERAINT PUGHE	Lighting
SHAUN DAVEY	Music

"Electrically alert to all its clashing dissonances, Sam Mendes's production at Stratford locates the drama in a temporal no man's land. The stars of the evening, though, are the Swan Theatre itself and Simon Russell Beale as the cankered, railing chorus-figure Thersites. With its sheer, stacked-up galleries and debating-hall feel, the Swan is the perfect venue for a play which offers colliding perspectives on the action. Mendes makes brilliant use of the place. Hunchbacked, rheumy-eyed and kitted out in a rancid flasher's mac, Beale's Thersites makes your average dosser look like a fitness fanatic. Fat, beaky features emerging from a tight-fitting bonnet, he also reminds you of an anthropomorphised storybook animal – Toad, say, dressed up as the washerwoman. Perhaps this is not inapt, since animal imagery features prominently in this scabrous, reductivist commentary on love and war. A hilarious, scuttling sadomasochist, Beale seems to get an illicit kick out of being routinely kicked. Vocally, he produces what Sir Fopling Flutter, after a century of skid row, might sound like in a play by Berkoff. [...] By the end of Troilus and Cressida, *the play has disillusioned you about almost everything. Except, that is, about the ability of genius to make some artistic sense of the disorder. Or, in this case, about the dazzling promise of the 24-year-old director."*

(Paul Taylor, The Independent, 30 April 1990)

Troilus and Cressida is a play fraught with the most extraordinary dissonances, not least of all in the Trojan Wars that provide its historical context, but also in the clash of comedy and tragedy and the conflict of high and low art forms. In the 1609 Quarto the title page for the play categorised it as a history, but in the 1623 Folio it was ordered as the first of the tragedies. To complicate matters further the Epistle to the reader described is as a comedy.

In addition to its questionable tonality, which can lead to vastly different productions, the play also accommodates multiple narrative arcs. Although the titular roles of Troilus and Cressida are obviously important, this is one of the rare Shakespeare plays, comparable with Chekhov, that has many 'lead' roles and where there appears to be a different central character depending on what production you go and see. Sam remembers vividly, "Howard Davies' production in the mid-80s at the RSC, which was the last time the show had been staged there prior to our production, where Pandarus was played by Clive Merrison and he was definitely the defining voice of that production. He began and ended it. Simon somehow came to capture the tone of my production. I think that it's fair to say that in the finished piece, Thersites was the defining voice."

Frequently when approaching productions with significant leading roles directors will begin to construct the general tone and feel of their piece around their chosen actor, sometimes to the extent to which choosing the actor is the first decision that is made for a given script. In essence, the collaboration on a particular play can begin with the offer of the role which, if the role is central enough, is an offer of a production shaped around the actor's performance in that part.

It is not therefore uncommon for a series of preliminary meetings to take place between the director and lead actor as key early decisions and ideas are formed. This ensures that the collaborators have a shared vision and understanding of what they will be working towards when rehearsals start.

Sam and Simon first met at the Barbican in 1989 in what Sam describes as "a sort of arranged marriage" organised by Terry Hands, the then Artistic Director of the RSC. "He said 'If you're going to be doing *Troilus and Cressida* then these are the people that I'd like you to cast. I'd like you to find a role for Ralph Fiennes and for Simon Russell Beale.' Now, looking back on it, you think 'Lucky me,' being *forced* to cast Ralph Fiennes and Simon Russell Beale. 'Oh dear, I've managed to find roles for them against my will!'"

Fiennes was returning to the RSC to play Berowne in *Love's Labour's Lost* and Edmund in Nicholas Hytner's production of *King Lear*. He had previously appeared there as Henry VI in Adrian Noble's *Plantagenets* season in which Sam had seen him and was very impressed. As for Simon, "I was sort of handed him in a weird way as one of the up-and-coming "comic" stars of the RSC. I saw him in the Restoration season playing Lord Are in *Restoration* by Edward Bond and I thought that he was fantastic but I did think of him as fundamentally a comic actor. It's partly to do with his shape and also because I'd seen him make such a wonderful job playing a fop. He'd played a series of fops in that season. That had been the only one I'd seen but I knew that they'd all been very good."

The initial meeting consisted of a walk around the Barbican centre which was at that time the permanent London home of the RSC. They browsed the bookshop, had a cup of tea and chatted. Sam recalls that he "instinctively liked Simon. We talked the same language. We were both educated at Cambridge and, rather boringly, we had the same pool of literary references. I never thought that this was the beginning of a long and fruitful relationship, one never does. I just thought, 'What a nice guy, and I'm sure he's going to be good as Thersites.'" Other than their first meeting and the phone call to offer the role of Thersites, Sam and Simon did not meet again until the first day of rehearsals on *Troilus and Cressida*.

At the time Simon claimed that *Troilus and Cressida* was "a tiny bit of a watershed year for me. I was desperate to do these sorts of parts and now I'm petrified. It's like my bluff being called. In *Some Americans Abroad*, an RSC production directed by Roger Michell, I spent rehearsals clutching at the shoulder strap of my bag because my hands automatically assumed a Restoration pose. I'm afraid that Thersites will start as Danny [from *Some Americans Abroad*]." In the end result, Simon had absolutely nothing to be worried about. "As it happened it transpired to be one of the most glorious experiences of my acting life. It was a wondrous production. It was the most amazing cast, looking back and then there was Sam and there was definitely a sense that I thought 'Yes I understand the way that this person is talking' and I hoped that he understood the way that I talked. I don't remember any special relationship developing immediately; we were all sort of in it together."

This included the designer Anthony Ward, who created the first of the blank canvasses in which Sam and Simon worked: a bare wooden boards environment open to a mixture of the historical and the modern, reflecting the striking dissonances in the play, and prefiguring Tim Hatley's similar design for *Richard III*.

Ward was also a vital component of the co-authorship of the character that Sam and Simon created. "You could say that Thersites was like putting together a Frankenstein's monster," suggests Sam. "He was created from the body parts of other people. You have on the one hand a flasher's mac and a string vest and then there were two things that were important to both us: one was surgical gloves. I know it sounds crazy, but the sense that under all of these layers there was a scrofulous, infected, pox-ridden, leprous, suppurating person was very important to the sense of who Thersites was. He is infected, he is diseased. Then, secondly, a stroke of genius arrived out of a meeting between Simon and Anthony, and holding up Thersites' trousers was an MCC tie."

"The combination of this created the sense that Thersites had once been this public schoolboy, a beaten fag at public school kicked around by the prefects and forced into having cold showers and buggered and God knows what. Somehow this whole history was unlocked for the character through the design. Now this vast intelligence is being used as a batman for Ajax, the most relentlessly stupid of the Greek Warriors. That was unlocked by that one small design detail – or, not so much unlocked, as it was given freedom. It's okay to be a posh person being forced to do a menial task."

What one learns from that in terms of Simon is that he is like a magpie, taking all of the tiny details and pulling them together to make them part of the complete fabric of the character. "The image I have of him is like a hamster. He will take the nut of the idea and he'll store it in the pouch in his cheek and he'll say, 'Oh, I'll have that, I'll store that for later,' and you'll see his little eyes light up. You know he hasn't consumed it yet, but you know he's going to take it into a corner and hoard it. Then he's going to take out all of these acorns and make them into a full meal. The difference between him and an ordinary actor is that he'll make them into something far fuller than you ever thought possible when you fed him the idea. In a funny way, all of these roles have felt like that with Simon. You feed ideas and gradually this thing that was an accumulation of good ideas becomes this complete person. That's Simon talent."

Thersites enters for the first time in Act II, Scene 1, looking utterly frustrated and downtrodden, carrying Ajax's breakfast on a huge silver platter. He lays it on a table and lifts the lid to reveal an array of beautifully cooked full English breakfast. He then hacked up an enormous gob of spit and spat right into the middle of the breakfast and exited without saying a word. Then Ajax entered and started eating it and Thersites simply stood and watched him. "It was the best entrance that I've ever given anyone in a single play and it remains so." The relationship is established straight away in the minds of the audience without a word being spoken. "Richard Ridings played it absolutely brilliantly. Ajax was this huge, vast, 6ft 6in rugby player. And if you give Simon an idea like that and see his eyes light up, you know that he's going to turn it into something special."

The running joke that exists between them about the tension between vulgarity and classicism originated during *Troilus and Cressida*. Sam had the idea that Thersites should have a wireless gramophone. "I said that instead it should be like the radio that you have in the kitchen. A wireless gramophone was far too sentimental. I remember the adverse happening to me and Sam slapping down some piece of vulgarity. We joked then about our balance of Puritanism and vulgarity being in synch. Ever since then we've tended to be opposing at various points and tempering one another. I wasn't always the vulgar one and he wasn't always the Puritan or vice versa."

In many ways the mixture of the vulgar and the classical is epitomised by Thersites as a whole. Once the decision was made about the radio, the subsequent decision was about what the music playing on it should be. Simon wanted Frank Sinatra or Nat King Cole singing *Lover Man*. "Unfortunately that has words in it so you can't use it. It just sounded odd: that funny mixture of romanticism and cynicism with Thersites is somehow encapsulated in the fact that he carries around Frank Sinatra's *Songs for Swinging Lovers!*," he says with a chuckle.

Another long-standing joke also started on this first production. Simon's ability to lock into words, phrases and rhythms can sometimes be directed to the most unlikely lines in the play. "He'll do it on the wrong line, or on ten lines, or he'll even play the good reviews which is the other thing that I'll tell him not to do. He does that sometimes. He has his moments."

In *Troilus and Cressida*, there is the line "The sun borrows of the moon when Diomed keeps his word." For some inexplicable reason, perhaps the beauty and the poetry of it, Simon attached himself to this line. "He definitely delivered it as if it were freighted with all sorts of hidden meanings. The audience wondered why on earth we were spending so much time on a minor character, but Diomedes is not really key. Simon was determined so I asked him to ease up on that line."

"By the time I'd been doing the production for a year and a half I was delivering the line with this huge portentousness," Simon admits. "Sam said 'Why are you doing that line as if it's the meaning of the play? That's become the regular joke: when I decide to 'do a line like the meaning of the play.' That even came up as recently as *The Winter's Tale*. I can't remember which line it was but Sam said 'Why are you doing that line like it's the meaning of the play? Mind, you... it is the meaning of the play!' So I got away with that one."

When Simon was able to wring the full linguistic delight out of the words, he did so magnificently, particularly with Thersites' longest and most vitriolic lists.

THERSITES The rotten diseases of the south, the guts-gripping ruptures, catarrhs, loads o'gravel in the back, lethargies, cold palsies, raw eyes, dirt-rotten livers, wheezing lungs, bladders full of imposthume, sciaticas, limekilns i' th' palm, incurable bone-ache, and the rivelled fee-simple of the tetter, take and take again such preposterous discoveries!

(V.i.16-22)

"It's a brilliant line and Simon delivered it breathtakingly. Thersites' lists were delivered like music by Simon but all of them got enormous laughs. That was the first sign for me that Simon was able to craft great tracts of contorted Shakespearean verse or prose and make them comprehensible through sheer sense of rhythm and music."

THERSITES To be a dog, a mule, a cat, a fitchew, a toad, a lizard, an owl, a puttock, or a herring without a roe, I would not care; but to be Menelaus, I would conspire against destiny.

(V.i.58-63)

"That brought the house down every night and I can tell you there was not one person in that audience who could tell you absolutely what every one of those things was but the shape of it, the music of it, he landed it perfectly. That is an unbelievable gift. I don't know anyone else that can do that in the same way."

"It was a brilliant class thing that Simon managed to pull off which is to use his own understanding of class and his own background. The bitterness came from the sense of 'I'm so much better than this. Look at my learning. Look at the way I can list these things.' He's not a working class character, Thersites, but he's been trapped into doing a job."

From his silent entrance with Ajax's breakfast through the rhythms of his vitriolic tracts, Simon's Thersites was a brilliant balance of verbal dexterity and non-verbal images. The reviewers latched on to one such moment in *Troilus and Cressida*. Thersites watched Cressida's betrayal of Troilus to Diomed from the upper gallery of the Swan Theatre's tiered back wall. As she exited, she left behind a veil on stage.

Sam encouraged Simon to smell the veil. "Smell the life that you will never have. Smell the beauty of the perfume." Thersites came down from the gallery and took a deep sniff of the discarded garments. It seemed to momentarily disturb and confuse him as if even Thersites was not immune to pity after all and delivered what could arguably be 'the line of the play': "Lechery, lechery! Still wars and lechery! Nothing else holds fashion."

"He made it something amazing. He made it something full of longing, loss and disappointment. Lechery wasn't just about these hideous people. It was about the things that drive people to madness. I have been driven to madness. I wish I were driven to madness. It was all sorts of things bound into this one line."

It may be more of 'the line of the play' than "The sun borrows of the moon when Diomed keeps his word," but after reading the aforementioned reviews Simon was delivering both lines with equal portentousness. "The next time I saw it, it took about five times as long!" Sam remembers. His note to Simon was "It was great before you read the reviews, which by the way were great, but calm it down a little bit."

During Act V of the play, devoted predominantly to the battle sequences, Thersites was kept on stage for longer than he appears in the text, another demonstration that in Sam's production it was Simon as Thersites who had the 'defining voice.'

Indeed, it could be argued that often Simon takes the role in the play that best demonstrates Sam's point of view on the production. Just as Thersites defined *Troilus and Cressida*, so the superior and remote Ariel would define the 'super-cool' *Tempest* and Malvolio in *Twelfth Night* would most fully epitomise how love can alter how a person behaves in society. In some ways these characters, particularly Thersites and Ariel, operate as choric figures, existing both within and outside the action, able to connect directly with the audience.

"I think Sam would probably deny that, but in the early work, perhaps there was an element of me playing the characters that represented Sam's view. I always think *Troilus and Cressida* is a young man's play. It has that sort of angry, cynical, the whole-world's-going-to-hell-in-a-handcart, teenage feel and it suited Sam." That anger and cynicism was certainly channelled through the vitriol of Simon's performance.

Simon finds the comparison between Thersites and Ariel interesting, but refers to them as 'the solitary characters' rather than as choric figures, believing them to be singled out by the actions and their demeanour rather than through any directorial decision. "Thersites is isolated by his own behaviour in this case, as is Malvolio, as is Ariel but Ariel because he's a different creature and because he's on stage all the time, he became choric but in a completely read-into-it-what-you-will way."

For some productions, it would be impossible for the lead actor's performance not to define the production, particularly with a role the size of *Richard III* where the actor's personality and approach to the part is the prime way of accessing and categorising the production. For *The Winter's Tale* too, it would be unlikely for us to identify with any production of the play without us understanding the action predominantly through Leontes' eyes. It is his perspective of marital infidelity that is offered directly to the audience.

"I think *The Winter's Tale* looks like a commentary only by virtue of Leontes being such a large part in the first half. It probably did seep into Ariel as a choric figure in a way that was so blank that it was up to the audience to determine what that meant, whereas with Thersites it was absolutely in your face."

Lechery, lechery! Still wars and lechery! Nothing else holds fashion.

RICHARD III

"Simon led the audience laughing into the heart of darkness"

RICHARD III by WILLIAM SHAKESPEARE
FIRST PERFORMANCE: The Other Place, Stratford Upon Avon, 5 August 1992
SUBSEQUENT PERFORMANCES:
Meadowside Leisure Centre, Burton-on-Trent, 29 September – 3 October
Macclesfield Leisure Centre, Cheshire, 6 – 10 October
The Dome, Doncaster, 13 – 17 October
Stratford Park Leisure Centre, Stroud, 20 – 24 October
Truro School, Cornwall, 27 – 31 October
North Devon Leisure Centre, Barnstaple, 3 – 7 November
Rainbow Leisure Centre, Middlesbrough, 10 – 14 November
The Sands Centre, Carlisle, 17 – 21 November
The Whitla Hall, Belfast, 24 – 28 November
South Lakeland Leisure Centre, Kendal, 1 – 5 December
Black Lions Sports Centre, Gillingham, 8 – 12 December
Braintree Leisure Centre, Essex, 15 – 19 December
Donmar Warehouse, London, 14 January 1993 – 20 February
The Globe, Tokyo, 22 February – 6 March
Schouwburg Theatre, Rotterdam, 11 – 13 March
Swan Theatre, Stratford-Upon-Avon, 18 March – 1 May

CAST

SIMON RUSSELL BEALE	Gloucester
ANNABELLE APSION	Lady Anne
MARK BENTON	Dorset / Murderer / Ely
STEPHEN BOXER	Buckingham
SIMON DORMANDY	Clarence / Ratcliffe
MIKE DOWLING	Edward IV / Lord Mayor
KATE DUCHÊNE	Queen Elizabeth
SAM GRAHAM	Brakenbury
ELLIE HADDINGTON	Duchess of York
CHRISTOPHER HUNTER	Lord Hastings / Urswick
MARK LEWIS JONES	Richmond / Grey
CHERRY MORRIS	Queen Margaret
MICHAEL PACKER	Rivers / Tyrrel
DANIEL RYAN	Catesby

CREATIVE TEAM

SAM MENDES	Director
TIM HATLEY	Designer
PAUL PYANT	Lighting
PADDY CUNNEEN	Composer
TERRY KING	Fight Director

"One day, I suppose, the gifted young director Sam Mendes will come a cropper, but there's not sign of it yet... [H]is staging of Richard III *at the Other Place Stratford-upon-Avon is a model of clarity and intelligence. As is in almost all of Mendes's work, there is a real freshness of approach here that never lapses into gimmickry. Mendes's staging is timeless... Nor is there any attempt to force a rigid, limiting interpretation on the play – instead almost every scene is played with a real attention to detail and a marvellously alert eye for comedy, leaving the audience to draw its own conclusions. More than almost any other Shakespeare play, the success of* Richard III *finally depends on the actor playing the title role. It's like a concerto, with Richard as the solo instrument and the other characters as the orchestra, and Simon Russell Beale doesn't strike a single false note... From the magnificent opening speech, delivered with an irresistible mixture of humour and contempt, Beale makes the part emphatically his own... Squat, hairless and plump, with an impressive hump beneath his overcoat, he stumps around on his stick looking every inch the "poisonous bunch-backed toad". His face is fleshly and corrupt, his manner horribly insinuating. Despite all your best intentions, you find yourself, like Lady Anne in the sinister wooing scene, surrendering to his vile personality, both repelled and enthralled."*

(Charles Spencer, The Daily Telegraph, 13 August 1992)

Sam had long wanted to do a production of *Richard III* and was looking for the actor who he could work with to take on this famous and immense role, second in length only to Hamlet. "After Simon's Thersites I thought to myself 'What am I waiting for?'" So, he arrived at Simon's thirtieth birthday with the job offer as a present. "Then, of course, my bowels did move. I thought that's absolutely fine. Spot on. Right, let's go." This bowel movement barometer is Simon's way of expressing the peculiar brand of euphoria that hits any actor that has been cast in an exciting role in a major production: a blend of delight, anticipation and terror.

In the "timeless staging" Sam and his designer Tim Hatley had created a genuine blank canvas of bare boards where a mixture of time periods could intersect. Traditional costumes were juxtaposed against bowler hats, cigars and anglepoise lamps where necessary; any image that stretched an idea to its maximum point and conveyed the correct information to the audience. The maximum point is the extreme to which you can push an idea; it's one step before you're doing something 'over the top' or, as Sam describes it, "the point before it breaks." Simon was intent that the Richard that inhabited this world would be a grotesque, but not a psychopath. He was someone who had "a very deeply developed sense of morality that he chooses to ignore. He's got a certain sex appeal."

Critics variously compared the end result to Dickensian characters Magwitch and Wackford Squeers, the wrestler Big Daddy, Mr Punch, Mussolini, Frankie Howerd, the Grendel, and a saturnine cartoon straight from the pages of Viz magazine. Yet Charles Spencer's review in the Telegraph made this production synonymous with one of Shakespeare's own bestial images: if Antony Sher's 1984 portrayal was "the bottled spider" then Simon's 1992 take was certainly "the poisonous bunch-backed toad."

Starting with one of Sam's initial images, this Richard was heard before he was seen, as the percussive sound of his spindly walking cane met with the bare boards and the "toad" delivered the famous opening speech in the discreet glow of a rehearsal lamp. His tone was informative and naturalistic, as if he was conversing directly to each audience member in the intimate auditoria that the show was designed for on its small-scale tour. Only as he reached the word "lute" and his description of the dalliances that his deformity prevents him from indulging in does the underlying anger creep through.

Taking another cue from this initial speech, Sam introduced a recurring sound effect into the production. Richard claims that his body is such that "dogs bark at me as I halt by them." This meant that many of the entrances that Simon made during the first half were punctuated by a canine cacophony as if he'd literally had to fight his way through the pack to gain admittance into the building.

Simon's ability to introduce "darkness into the light and light into the darkness" has been one of the techniques he has utilised throughout his career and it was already in evidence in his portrayal of Richard. Indeed, "His Hamlet was one of the funniest I've ever seen and yet it was also the most moving. He's not scared of laughter. I thought that it was very successful in *Richard III*. Simon led the audience laughing into the heart of darkness."

The audience were not the only ones to be seduced. In the famous wooing scene, Lady Anne was won over by his mild manners and his apparent sense of the pious and the holy; Richard's eyes were continually raised to heaven as if there was a strong awareness that the attempted tryst was taking place in the sight of God.

RICHARD If thy revengeful heart cannot forgive,
Lo, here I lend thee this sharp-pointed sword,
Which if thou please to hide in this true breast
And let the soul forth that adoreth thee
I lay it naked to the deadly stroke
And humbly beg the death upon my knee.

(I.2.173-178)

The character was also endowed with Simon's own intelligence and speed of analysis. In this production, when Richard proffered his naked breast for Anne to stab as a ploy to demonstrate his utter devotion, she went so far as to nick his chest with the blade. Richard was momentarily disorientated by the drawn blood but then swiftly reappraised the situation, and analysed how this latest apparent 'setback' could be used to his advantage.

"With Richard III the actor and the character are both fully in control right from the start. They mischievously begin to test the boundaries of their power," Sam insists. "Richard III tells the audience, 'I'm just going to see if this works. I'm just going to see if I can get Clarence locked up. Oh, that worked. I'm just going to see if I can persuade Lady Anne to fall for me. Oh, that worked too. Goodness me,

I'm much more in control than I thought I was.' The play begins with a character not overreaching. He's not yet in crisis."

When starting work on the production Simon had the idea that *Richard III* was "a rather simple show following one man but perplexed by these cocky little boys and prophetically astute queens." The "cocky little boys" in question being the two Princes whom Simon believes Richard "absolutely loathes. He finds them infuriating and he barely communicates with them." When he and Buckingham deliberately meet the Princes in the absence of the rest of their uncles in Act III, Scene 1, the younger sibling breaks an infamous taboo by climbing upon Richard's shoulders:

YOUNG YORK You mean to bear me not to bear with me.
Uncle, my brother mocks both you and me
Because that I am little like an ape
He thinks that you should bear me on your shoulders.
(III.i.128-131)

It is a moment that frequently leads to an anguished cry from Richard leaving Buckingham and others to calm the situation. Instead Simon allowed a long pause for Richard to suppress his utter fury, before breaking the tension with exaggerated frivolity, high jinks and a manic piggyback ride. It was a chilling reminder of the danger that lurks beneath the surface of the comic flair.

For the scene when Richard hears that the murder of the princes has been successful, Simon was particularly pleased with the size of the venues that the production toured to after its initial run in the intimate auditorium of The Other Place. "It meant that you could scale everything down to a very low level. The scene when the Princes have been killed in the Tower, for instance, was a very quiet scene and a very depressing scene. It's also a great release for him too, I think." This, of course, was the scene that featured the 'Hilda Ogden moment' as Richard sniffed the pyjamas of the infants that Tyrrel had brought from the crime scene to assure the monarch of their deaths.

His contempt of the princes was extended to every other character that he encountered. He informed Lady Anne of his intent that the princes should die directly to her face shortly before informing her of her own imminent demise. He was constantly astounded at how so many people could be so easily taken in by all of his plots and machinations, not least of all the citizens, whom he must ultimately convince to accept him as their ruler. “That was an interesting discussion, about how gullible Shakespeare makes his citizens, and how convincing Richard should be. You don’t know quite what to do with that scene, whether to play it straight or ironic. I don’t think that it’s the most successful scene that Shakespeare wrote.”

Lady Anne is one of the many “prophetically astute queens”, in the play. The Lancastrian Queen Margaret is greeted on her first appearance with a groan of weary familiarity. Her own personal history is bound up intimately with Richard as she counts her husband and her son amongst his many victims. She is the person that invokes the most insults and bestial imagery in describing Richard, including devil, villain, cacodemon, hog, dog (twice), spider and then, of course, “poisonous bunch-backed toad.”

Her prophecies seem to indicate that she is aware of the lineage that Richard intends, from her husband Henry VI, through Richard’s own brothers and their heirs to himself. When Richard sees the corpse of Henry VI he hovers over it like a mortician examining a case on the slab. When he carelessly sits on the throne before he is entitled, he leaps out of it with a faux apologetic expression “as if he’s suddenly been goosed.” No sooner has she departed the scene than Richard initiates the next stage of his coup to bring Margaret’s philosophy to fulfilment. When a pair of hired assassins arrive he greets them “with a jovial ‘How now, my hardy, stout, resolved mates?’ like a lord of the manor admitting a pair of plumbers.”

The humour and joviality continue through the Council Chamber scene (Act III, Scene 4) and in the dispatch of Hastings, the Lord Chamberlain and a staunch supporter of putting the eldest of the princes onto the throne. Richard’s suggestion to Buckingham that they should “Chop off his head”, if Hastings will not support them, has already been delivered in a previous scene in such a laissez-faire manner that it’s hardly surprising that Richard clutches Hastings’ head in the Council meeting as if he’s measuring it for the executioner’s block. As part of the ruse that is Hastings’ ultimate undoing, Richard smothers his own closely cropped head with the Bishop of Ely’s strawberries in the brazen pretence that he’s been attacked.

One of Sam’s favourite moments in the production was when Hastings’ head was delivered to Richard in a brown paper parcel in the image that he had lifted directly from *Barton Fink*. Richard plunged his walking cane into the package. The resulting squelching sound used to provoke a huge reaction from the audience and as Richard withdrew his cane, he wiped the residue from off the end. "The audience would let out this huge 'Uggghhh...' but it was all through suggestion. There obviously wasn't a head inside. It was a melon!"

Many people regard Richard's anointment as the major turning point of the play, when he has actually achieved all that he set out to do in the opening speech. "Once the crown is on his head it's not what he expected it to be. He wasn't born to be king. He's really in the wrong job and that's what kills him." In this production his entrance as king at the beginning of Act IV was a marked difference from the self-congratulatory yell that he lets out at the end of Act III as if delighted that it's "mission accomplished".

Simon wanted to try and make the coronation "as magnificent as possible." Although the make-up image had been cut, the designer Tim Hatley had given the character "a very, very beautiful, long, blue ermine cloak. He was a bully-boy monster, but he had this very big blue cloak." Thus Richard King III entered, again from the darkness and through the auditorium as at the top of the first half, this time with a pulsing percussive fanfare replacing the tapping of his walking cane.

Just before Richard reached the throne he tripped and fell and fought off anyone that attempted to help him. Eventually he realised that he couldn't get up by himself. As Sam recalls "Richard fell and then he wouldn't let anyone assist him and he finally had to accept that Buckingham was the only one that he'd allow to help him." "Give me thy hand," now became more than a show of favour or gratitude, it was a panicked injunction for aid.

KING RICHARD Stand all apart. Cousin of Buckingham –

BUCKINGHAM My gracious sovereign?

KING RICHARD Give me thy hand.

(IV.ii.1-3)

This is another example of pushing ideas to their maximum point. Here, what appears to be an innocent exchange of ceremonial procedure on the page was thrillingly reinvented through the investigation in the rehearsal room. The fall became the perfect visual metaphor for Richard's descent from euphoria into anguish.

"He's genuinely immoral, not amoral. Yet gaining power doesn't make him happy, and he also loses his skill; that seems to be a regular pattern. You see these really empty people at the end. Richard at the end is extremely lonely – in fact, Adrian Noble said to me that he's the loneliest man Shakespeare wrote. There's a wonderful scene in *Richard III* when he tries to rebuild his family by marrying his niece."

These lapses of control indicate the potential for vulnerability within the monster. In a flip scene to the earlier wooing scene of Lady Anne, Richard attempts to seduce Queen Elizabeth to give up her daughter so that Richard can marry her, uniting the Houses of York and Lancaster. In the Lady Anne scene, every tactic that Richard employs is a ploy designed to achieve the objective of claiming Anne for his wife. In the Lady Anne scene he succeeds, in the Queen Elizabeth he fails "though blissfully he thinks that he's won, even though he sort of knows that he's failed," says Simon with relish.

"Sam is very willing for me to try and find a softer edge to characters. He's very good about allowing my 'discoveries' to be discussed. I suddenly thought in this scene that this was Richard at his most genuine actually and not at his most devious. Richard's lines saying that if I do not marry your daughter it will be continued civil war are him at his most frightened."

KING RICHARD Without her, follows to myself and thee,
Herself, the land, and many a Christian soul,
Death, desolation, ruin, and decay.
It cannot be avoided but by this;
It will not be avoided but by this"

[IV.iv.408-411]

"I thought that this was a genuine appeal. It doesn't make him any more likeable but it means that it's not a ploy. Sam was very willing to allow me to do that."

In starting to allow Richard's genuine needs to come through, the level of control that the character exhibits at the start of the play was shown on the decline. This made the difficult transition into Richard facing his own conscience feel like a natural progression after he has attained the crown when, in so many other productions, it seems a largely implausible addendum. One critic wrote that "Beale creates a rapt, terrifying impression of a man finally confronted by his own innate evil."

As things finally come apart at the seams, the jokes and glee which Richard employed in murdering his way to a kingdom are now replaced with half-crazed laughter and desperation and all that remains is his inevitable demise in his final confrontation with the armies of Richmond. "The difficulty lies in the turning up the volume with the Battle of Bosworth Field but Sam had already done that with the entire Trojan Wars in *Troilus and Cressida* so I thought he could cope with Bosworth!"

In order to increase the volume, and the pace and the excitement, Sam took the decision to intercut Richard's oration to his army with Richmond's address to his faction, which Shaw once described as "pious twaddle," creating a dynamic pre-cursor to the fighting itself. Yet Sam will always remember the battle by the climatic encounter between Richmond and Richard as individuals. "It was an amazing fight at the end between the two of them: a sort of bestial fight in the mud."

THE TEMPEST

"I'm not going to fly, that would be visually ludicrous"

THE TEMPEST by WILLIAM SHAKESPEARE
FIRST PERFORMANCE: Royal Shakespeare Theatre, Stratford-upon-Avon, 5 August 1993

CAST

SIMON RUSSELL BEALE	Ariel
JOHANNA BENYON	Ceres
DAVID BIRRELL	Adrian
DAVID BRADLEY	Trinculo
MIKE BURNSIDE	Boatswain
RICHARD CLOTHIER	Francisco
VIRGINIA GRAINGER	Juno
PAUL GREENWOOD	Alonso
PETER GRIMES	Ensemble
SEAN HANNAWAY	Ensemble
JAMES HAYES	Antonio
CHRISTOPHER HUNTER	Sebastian
MARK LEWIS JONES	Ferdinand
MARK LOCKYER	Stephano
ALEC McCOWEN	Prospero
ROBIN PRATT	Ensemble
SIAN RADINGER	Iris
CHRISTOPHER ROBBIE	Master of the Ship
CLIFFORD ROSE	Gonzalo
DAVID TROUGHTON	Caliban
SARAH WEYMOUTH	Ensemble
SARAH WOODWARD	Miranda

CREATIVE TEAM

SAM MENDES	Director
ANTHONY WARD	Designer
PAUL PYANT	Lighting
SHAUN DAVEY	Music
TERRY JOHN BATES	Movement

"Sam Mendes's striking account of The Tempest *jerks into life when Simon Russell Beale's Ariel springs, jack-in-the-box-like, from this basket and claps his hands. [...] In putting Ariel right at the heart of things, the opening sequence is again indicative of the production's priorities throughout. While it wouldn't altogether be fair to retitle the show Ariel Pulls it Off, Simon Russell Beale's mesmeric performance as the spirit certainly seizes some of the dramatic supremacy [...] It's Russell Beale's Ariel who looks as though he could turn decidedly nasty. His far from sylph-like form crammed into a blue silk Mao suit, he pads about barefoot making 90-degree turns and looking like a Stepford Wives equivalent of Wishee Washee. God knows what his mind is picking up on its far-flung frequencies, but the beady, remote hauteur of his stare suggest that, compared with him, Jeeves is in the grip of gibbering inferiority complex. There are some eerily comic moments when his Ariel drops his prayerful, hands-raised, spirit-summoning pose and waits, with an inscrutable hint of insolent impatience, while Prospero offloads a thought or two on such subjects as the spirit's promised freedom."*

(Paul Taylor, *The Independent*, 13 August 1993)

It's late on a spring evening in 1993 and Sam Mendes is at the National Theatre on London's South Bank enjoying a drink with fellow directors Adrian Noble and Deborah Warner. Mendes' production of *Richard III* with Simon Russell Beale in the title role is already on tour and, following an exchange of complements and congratulations, the conversation turns to Mendes' forthcoming production of *The Tempest* for the Royal Shakespeare Company.

"Who have you got for Prospero?" asks Warner. "Alec McCowen." There's a nod of approval. In addition to being a multi Olivier award-winning actor, McCowen was originally a member of the RSC thirty years before when he played the Fool in Peter Brook's renowned production of *King Lear* opposite Paul Scofield, and therefore fulfils part of new Artistic Director Noble's vision of encouraging significant former members of the company to return for the new season.

"Who's going to do Caliban?" "Simon." From both Noble and Warner there is an acknowledgement without any excitement and even a distinct roll of the eyes. It's a damning verdict of a casting decision that feels too predictable, almost half-expected. Caliban seems to be just the inevitable next step in the series of characters the actor and the director have already undertaken together, following Thersites in *Troilus and Cressida* and Richard III.

When individuals frequently collaborate, there are a number of advantages: a high degree of trust is built; you learn each other's sensibilities; and a shorthand way of communicating can develop. Higher quality work can be achieved quicker. However, there is the danger that a routine will also emerge, that you get locked into a pattern, into repetition without progression: you become creatively stagnant.

Sam had already encountered an equally brutal indictment of his choice when he telephoned Simon to offer him the role. "It'll just be Richard III with no clothes. You know what you're going to get," he said, only half-joking. "I knew it was a great part, I knew it was a wonderful part and I knew that it had virtually the best speech in the play, which is a decent enough reason to take a part I suppose. I knew all of that. But it didn't make me think, 'Ah, right, this is something very unusual.'"

At this point, Sam was still being hailed as a wunderkind. Prior to starting work on *The Tempest* he had directed two successful and acclaimed productions for the RSC and was the founding Artistic Director of the Donmar Warehouse in London. His meteoric rise through the theatre industry was still in its ascendancy. As with all success, there is the ever present prospect of failure and many critics and individuals were already anticipating Sam's first false move. Hitting a plateau in creativity, even early in the casting process, could be the only excuse his critics needed.

Sheer terror was absolutely the sensation Simon experienced when Sam contacted him to tell him that he'd rethought the casting for *The Tempest* and that he no longer wanted Simon to play Caliban. The role now on offer was both a casting risk and a far more interesting prospect: Ariel, the spirit of air who serves Prospero. "It never occurred to me to do Ariel. But having been given it and having had that reaction of 'Wow. That is going to be a terrible mistake or that is going to be interesting.' Having decided to do it then you had to make some statement about it. I mean, I was 14 and a half stone... there's no way... that I'm a creature of air. I did say 'I'm not going to fly, that would be visually ludicrous.'"

Alec McCowen laughed when he heard about the casting change. "I'm going to have so much fun saying 'delicate Ariel.'" Sam and Simon were both aware that they were going to have to make some sort of statement with this character. It was an unexpected role for an unconventional leading actor, yet it was certainly a far more exciting proposition.

Of course, these sorts of creative predicaments can produce imaginative responses that stay with the character for the duration of the production. Sam always knew that he wanted Ariel to be a permanent presence, obeying Prospero's every command and performing each of his tasks perfectly, including bringing characters, props and pieces of set onto the stage. Through the rehearsal process, Ariel developed into a sort of omnipresent stage manager, which left Simon with a huge number of things to do throughout the show.

This meant that part of his costume was causing him discomfort as he was attempting to complete all of the tasks that he had been set. "I originally had a costume with shoes and socks but I felt the shoes and socks weren't right and I asked if I could be barefoot. You get that very elastic way of walking and the sense of contact with the environment around you. And that was just because I didn't like the shoes, they were slipping off my feet. These are entirely practical things." Ultimately, Ariel appeared barefoot throughout the production, in a blue Mao suit, designed by Anthony Ward.

During one of the first run-throughs of *The Tempest*, about three quarters of the way through the rehearsal process, Simon was preparing to undertake the full journey of the character, including all of the character's tasks. "Ariel had to do all the work. Prospero stood there looking magnificent while Ariel was working his tits off: bringing characters on, large sunflowers on. I thought to myself just concentrate and don't hurry, a bit like playing the piano; don't panic when you get to a difficult passage, just keep cool. I was also trying to give the impression of [Ariel] being weightless." So, Ariel made his diligent way through the run in a sort of slow motion.

Crucially, this was both a pragmatic approach and an artistic decision on Simon's part. With so many tasks to do within a scene, he was attempting to conserve energy by moving at a slower pace. Having avoided the 'visually ludicrous' choice of being flown in on wires, the slower pace was also a way of giving the impression of zero gravity. Sam had taken note of this during the run and found it incredibly interesting. "It's either going to be really, really, really dull, or you can slow it down further and it could be brilliant. We could have a semblance of a creature there." They took the decision to slow Ariel's pace down even further.

When forced to define their process, actors often have to resort to language about 'working from the inside out' or 'from the outside in.' Some actors begin from the interior, exploring what a character feels, how he or she thinks, how he or she behaves and therefore how he or she appears both publicly and privately. The alternative approach is to begin with a visual picture, imagining how the character appears and using exterior stimuli like costume to induce a physiological response to arrive at how the character feels. As Ariel is not a human being the parameters of the intellectual landscape and the starting point for a line of thought can be difficult to grasp. Ariel is very much an example of Sam and Simon working 'from the outside in.'

Having established this incredibly slow, elastic way of walking, Simon started to feel a sense of Ariel's resistance to the tasks he was completing and a defiant imperiousness. Armed with this feeling, Simon returned to the text and became obsessed with the number of times that Prospero tantalises Ariel with the prospect of freedom. How would Ariel feel if this bribe had been continuing for the entire twelve years that Prospero had been on the island? Simon also became very interested in some evidence in the text which suggests that the spirits of the island, which include Ariel, would not all seek retribution for Prospero suffering misfortune, if they were not controlled by his magic.

CALIBAN All the infections that the sun sucks up
From bogs, fens, flats, on Prosper fall, and make him
By inch-meal a disease! His spirits hear me,
And yet I needs must curse. But they'll nor pinch,
Fright me with urchin-shows, pitch me i'th'mire,
Nor lead me like a firebrand in the dark
Out of my way, unless he bid'em.

(*The Tempest*, II.ii.1-7)

"It's usually dismissed as Caliban's wish fulfilment but I wondered what would happen if it were true. Perhaps Caliban knows. I remember we had a sort of union meeting: all of the spirits gathered around the grand piano in the rehearsal room and discussed what our attitudes towards our boss were. It came out as this blanket resentment."

Eventually this series of incidental discoveries and pragmatic choices begins to cohere into a complete character: a superior entity, resentfully completing his master's instructions to perfection, because he is trapped by Prospero's magical power. It's a significantly different approach to more traditional portrayals. "As it happens with Ariel, and it is something that I am proud of, it all came by mistake. It was a list of lucky chances. The way he looked... the reason why he moved so slowly... It was a series of funny accidents."

Mendes' production of *The Tempest* took place in a storybook set of folding flats, a picturesque cloudscape and giant sunflowers, but was far from a sentimental retelling. This was a very cool production of the play – in terms of temperature rather than fashion – led by McCowen's super-intelligent, super-meticulous and very remote Prospero.

This 'ice cold' centre also extended to Simon's imperious Ariel, a superior creature isolated because of his difference. As a member of the audience, you had to read into his actions as you saw fit, there were no easy clues to read his passivity. There was the possibility that he took pleasure being able to do his tasks well, but then there was the sense that he was genetically pre-programmed to do this, that he couldn't do them badly. His tense power-struggle with Prospero and the ever-present promise of freedom, only added to the sheer cool of the production.

The first of these many tasks that we saw Ariel perform was setting the titular tempest in motion. Ariel was the first character on stage, emerging from a toy box basket and starting the entire performance. Even though Ariel doesn't appear in Act I, Scene 1 in Shakespeare's text, this is the first of many instances where Sam added Ariel into a scene as a stage-managing spirit, shepherding other characters and moving props. In the production, therefore, Ariel was present in scenes that do not feature him in the script, or appeared on stage long before his written entrance; for example the clown scenes between Caliban, Stephano and Trinculo (II.2 and III.2) and the conspiracy between Sebastian and Antonio amidst the marooned court.

On Ariel's first scripted entrance, in Act I, Scene 2, the stage is bathed in a blue light to suggest a different frequency of existence. Ariel recounted the events of the tempest that we have seen him put in motion before being told that there is a limited amount of time with which to complete further tasks. The following exchange is made all the more believable when conducted between a remote Prospero and an imperious Ariel:

ARIEL Is there more toil? Since thou dost give me pains,
Let me remember thee what thou hast promised,
Which is not yet performed me.

PROSPERO How now? Moody?
What is't thou canst demand?

ARIEL My liberty.

(*The Tempest*, I.ii)

On the contrary, Ariel's potential capacity for such human emotions as pity and compassion are hinted at in Simon's delivery of Ariel's song, "Full fathom five", at the end of the scene. His tenor voice, trained through his time as a chorister at St Paul's Cathedral and in his early years at the Guildhall School of Music and Drama, was another asset put to good use following the unconventional casting decision. It was an asset that Deborah Warner had mentioned to Sam when he was rethinking Simon's role.

There was one idea that would have seen Ariel performing in a very different fashion. During Act IV, Scene 1, the young lovers Miranda and Ferdinand are entertained by a masque of three goddesses – Iris, Ceres and Juno – which Ariel initiates following Prospero's instructions. Sam was alive to the potential editorial possibility that Ariel could play one of the goddesses. This was before the casting took place and Simon remains relieved that Sam abandoned the idea. "I think me in drag would be... not very magical."

Ariel was still required to initiate the masque. In this production, Sam was aware of the masque's inherent theatricality – a play within a play – and staged the masque in a box theatre which descended from the rig to the stage when Ariel raised his hands. "There was one very funny occasion when I lifted my hand during one performance... and nothing happened. When something goes wrong on stage I have a very acute sense of embarrassment. I try to have as few props as possible and when something goes wrong with a prop I hate it, and Sam can always see it from a mile off. My embarrassment in this instance was so acute that I just turned around – very slowly – and walked off the stage, leaving [Prospero, Miranda and Ferdinand] to think, 'what the hell is he doing?'"

It remains rare for Sam and Simon to have much contact about productions between the casting offer and the first day of rehearsals, but from time to time Sam will phone Simon with a small piece of information, such as a brief casting update. During pre-production on *The Tempest* he did call to gleefully announce "I've given you the best exit."

Right at the end of Act V, Scene 1, just before the play's epilogue, Prospero finally fulfils his promise to release his faithful servant. In the production, Ariel slowly glided across the stage in his elastic way of walking and opened a door in the back of the stage that had hitherto been concealed, revealing a new space of brilliant white light. Ariel stood in silhouette for a brief moment and then disappeared into this new plane of existence and to freedom.

Prior to this exit, there was a theatrical gesture that caused much controversy. Through the process of rehearsals, Ariel had become a very superior creature who performed his tasks to perfection but had a certain level of hatred towards his master, and was desperate for the freedom he had been promised for twelve years. During the final run of the play in rehearsals Sam approached Simon with a suggestion.

"I've had this idea that you should spit in Prospero's face at the end. I've told Alec and I haven't told anybody else."

"It was absolutely fascinating," recalls Simon. "After he told me I was free, I spat in his face. It was the single most extraordinary thing in terms of binding a cast together for debate that I've ever seen. People weren't expecting it and there were ones who loved it and ones who hated it and, funnily enough, it was divided almost entirely along the lines of the characters in the play. Ferdinand and Miranda hated it. Caliban loved it."

The spit was not as divisive in the production's critical reception, but the coolness of the production definitely reflected better on some actors than others. For the most part, the praise was once again heaped upon Simon, with Michael Billington noting in the Guardian that "What you lose in some areas you gain in others. Simon Russell Beale's excellent Ariel is like an ethereal, boiler-suited stage-manager hiding his rage behind a mask of passivity." However, the remoteness of Prospero left a sour taste in some critics' mouths. Simon is swift to say that this in no way affected his relationship with McCowen. Ariel's avuncular attitude came about as much in response to Alec as from Sam's suggestions and pragmatic discoveries. Alec remained enthusiastic about both Simon and the unconventional casting choice: "It's wonderful to be on stage with an actor of that authority and whom you can trust and experiment with. I guess he's unusual casting but it's such a relief to have an Ariel with whom I can have a really abrasive relationship instead of the usual rather wimpy little spirit."

Judging from the whoops and applause during curtain calls, Ariel and Caliban were also popular with the audience, though the controversial spit provoked a number of letters and even some heckling. "The famous spit caused a postbag – I've never had a postbag like it – although I did get irritated by letters that said 'A spirit wouldn't do that.' Because I felt like saying 'Well a spirit wouldn't sing or talk English or speak in blank verse or wear a Mao suit. I think we're in a sort of vague area here. We haven't got any first-hand experience of these things. Let's assume they can spit as well.'"

Eventually the spit was cut, though not due to any adverse comments. McCowen had initially been wary of Sam's suggestion, but since pursuing it had found it incredibly useful in hurting Prospero and allowing him a crack in his self-control in order to propel him into the epilogue. The spit had, however, become redundant. Ariel's imperiousness was evident and the power struggle was well established within the actors' handling of the text and the scenes. The defiant final gesture had outlived its use. It was mutually agreed that the spit should go. Simon now concedes that "it was a crude gesture. In the end, I think it was wrong. But I only say that through gritted teeth."

OTHELLO

"We were like mice menstruating together"

OTHELLO by WILLIAM SHAKESPEARE

FIRST PERFORMANCE: Cottesloe Theatre, National Theatre, 1 August 1997

SUBSEQUENT PERFORMANCES:

Salzburg Festival, Germany, 22 – 25 August 1997
Cottesloe Theatre, National Theatre, UK, 16 September 1997 (Press Night)
Herberger Theatre, Phoenix, Arizona, USA, 30 September – 4 October 1997
Dramatychny Theatre, Warsaw, Poland, 13 – 15 November 1997
Ginza Saison Theatre, Tokyo, Japan, 22 January – 8 February 1998
Seoul Arts Centre, Seoul, Korea, 11 – 20 February 1998
Academy of Performing Arts, Hong Kong, 24 February – 1 March 1998
Drama Academy, Beijing, China, 6 – 8 March 1998
State Opera House, Wellington, New Zealand, 19 – 23 March 1998
Majestic Theatre, Adelaide, Australia, 28 March – 2 April 1998
Brooklyn Academy of Music, New York, USA, 8 – 12 April 1998
Lyttelton Theatre, National Theatre, UK, 1 May – 13 June 1998

CAST

SIMON RUSSELL BEALE	Iago
MAUREEN BEATTIE	Emilia
DAVID HAREWOOD	Othello
JAMES HAYES	3rd Senator / Montano
JAMIE LEENE	4th Senator / 2nd Soldier
CRISPIN LETTS	Roderigo
FRANCIS MAGUIRE	Servant / 1st Soldier
KEN OXTOBY	1st Senator / 3rd Soldier
TREVOR PEACOCK	Brabantio / Gratiano
CLIFFORD ROSE	Duke / Lodovico
CLAIRE SKINNER	Desdemona
COLIN TIERNEY	Cassio
INDIRA VARMA	Bianca
FERGUS WEBSTER	2nd Senator / Clown

CREATIVE TEAM

SAM MENDES	Director
ANTHONY WARD	Designer
PAUL PYANT	Lighting
PADDY CUNNEEN	Music
JONATHAN BUTTERELL	Movement
PATSY RODENBURG	Voice Director
TERRY KING	Fight Director

"... Sam Mendes's brilliant new production. The main point is that Mendes, like Trevor Nunn before him, strengthens the tragedy by allowing it to grow out of an accumulation of domestic detail. But who is the central figure? Othello, fatally flawed by his mixture of self regard and insecurity? Or Iago, the active embodiment of evil? Mendes shrewdly suggests they are absolutely interdependent: that Iago's poison is able to work only because of some lurking doubt inside Othello. [...]Simon Russell Beale's Iago, who at one point illustrates his diabolical plan with the help of playing cards, reminds one of Auden's description of Iago as the joker in the pack. But Russell Beale is more than practical joker carrying out a scientific experiment: he memorably makes him a squat, shaven-headed, implicitly impotent nihilist, gnawed by the 'daily beauty' he sees in others' lives. There is a superb moment when he sits beside Othello whispering into his ear the words that prompt the general's epileptic fit: for this Iago, it's the ultimate symbol of destruction, possession and power."

(Michael Billington, *The Guardian*, 18 September, 1997)

Of all of Simon's performances which he has directed, Sam's personal favourite is Iago, because that was the character for which Simon transformed himself the most from the inside out. "It was the performance least dependent on effect. He went to a pretty dark place. I think for Simon, the self-hatred in Iago, the refusal of human contact and sex, the turning towards the dark in oneself, was absolutely something that he associated with at that point in his life. I thought Iago was an incredible performance, I mean really incredible."

Assumed to have been written during the period 1603-1604, *Othello* is the second of Shakespeare's late tragedies, sitting between *Hamlet* and *King Lear*. Yet unlike these monumental epics charting the fall of a central protagonist, *Othello,* though named after one character, is undoubtedly about its two central figures that are intrinsically linked. It is the dynamic between these two figures that forms the narrative arc of the play. There are no significant subplots and all the other characters are supporting this narrative thrust and are in relation to the central figures of Othello and Iago; this is particularly the case with their wives, Desdemona and Emilia.

Shakespeare's primary source for the drama was a short story in the *Hecatommithi* by Giraldi Cinthio though, according to Sam, who read the source material, the knowledge of this is of greater use to "learn about the play by seeing what [Shakespeare]'s left out rather than what he's put in." In editorialising details from the Cinthio, Shakespeare has removed information about Iago and Emilia's children for instance. In the source material Iago was considered to be a good father. Sam suggests that this is not a casual omission within the play, but a deliberate construction on Shakespeare's part in suggesting a tension in the relationship. Once again, the absence of children is of great significance within Shakespeare's work.

Sam was insistent upon the belief that Emilia wanted children. Her desire for children and the absence of them comes at the very root of the problems in their marriage and the unspoken conflict between them. "That's the reason that Emilia exposes him to be the villain," asserts Simon. "Discovering the idea about Emilia was a thrilling moment. Sounds pathetic, doesn't it? But the big question about Iago is why he did it. There has to be a consistent argument. There's no satisfactory answer, but the most satisfactory I've got is Emilia. And the thrill of that discovery was intellectual and emotional."

Male-female relationships are at the centre of the drama, within Iago and Emilia's childless marriage and of course within the love between Othello and Desdemona that slowly unravels with devastating consequences. The intense focus upon these relationships can be an exhausting and often bleak experience for the actors involved. "We were like mice menstruating together," recalls Simon. "The big four – the two main men and the two main women – all had moments of real unhappiness in this miserable story: because it is a *miserable* story."

With such concentration upon these relationships it was imperative that the pairs of actors worked well together and could quickly develop a shared history. Simon and Maureen Beattie (Emilia) were asked to construct a back story for how Iago and Emilia met. This is a marked difference from arriving at rehearsals without pre-conceptions or invented arrangements and from the independent conferences between Sam and Simon at the beginning of a day's rehearsal or an image-based way of working. "We probably didn't have time to go through the full details that we had worked out but Sam knew the basic outline: Emilia worked at the NAAFI [Navy, Army and Air Force Institutes] and Iago fancied her."

Sam's production was built on these small, almost undetectable details, not just from the source material and the subsequent omissions but also from the internal directions from within Shakespeare's text itself. All throughout Act I of *Othello* there are many eccentric pieces of timing. According to Sam, "Shakespeare telescopes time. It says that they arrive in Venice in three days, and in reality the journey took three weeks, we discovered in doing our research." Yet, where it is necessary and appropriate Shakespeare is very clear about times of day and places of setting. This matches Sam's appreciation for the play as a very domestic piece with a high degree of specificity. More so than in any other production, Sam spent time at the beginning of the rehearsal process ensuring that the actors were aware of and adhered to the language, the structure, the verse and the rhyme schemes.

Detail is a hallmark of this collaboration. In the critical reception of this production, many critics evoked their mutual sense of specificity and closely observed details as a shared value and a reason for the success of the show. In *The Times*, Jeremy Kingston was particularly impressed that the servants would bring on more glasses than were needed for the characters arriving in the scene, as the hosts would not have known how many guests would ultimately be present.

Until the twentieth century, *Othello* was one of Shakespeare's most popular tragedies, enjoying successful performances following its premiere at Whitehall on 1st November 1604, many of them indoors at the Blackfriars. There are far more textual references to interior rather than exterior scenes which may explain its success within a more intimate auditorium, and corresponds to Sam's understanding of the play as a domestic piece, ripe for the comparable environment of the Cottesloe.

Matching the mood of misery and deception and the period setting of the 1950s, Paul Pyant's initial lighting state for the opening moments of the production saw Iago and Roderigo navigating shafts of light and depths of shadow, evoking the *chiaroscuro* of film noir. This led the *Independent on Sunday* to dub the production 'Black and White and Noir all over.' "It was very noir-ish in China," says Simon slyly. "At one venue we only had two lamps."

Yet China provided the company with one of the most memorable experiences of the entire tour. In Beijing the auditorium was within a complex that contained the city's Drama Academy. "There were students banging on the doors trying to get in and a huge crush all around the theatre. The atmosphere was amazing," recalls Simon. "It also proved to me that Shakespeare is the most international of all writers."

Working within a dark overriding mood can sometimes take its toll on the actors. Simon remembers at one point he simply had to walk out of the rehearsal room. "I suspect it happens quite a lot with *Othello*. We all had a moment when we thought we couldn't cope with it anymore." On this occasion, during "Give me the ocular proof," David Harewood, as Othello, had thrust a gun into Iago's neck to emphasise the danger of the command.

"It was absolutely planned and expected but it hurt and I was pissed off. I just went 'I've had enough of this, I'm going to the loo,' and I walked off. I washed my face, I stormed for a bit and eventually I came back in. Sam just said 'I love it when you're angry' and then it was all okay." Although Sam diplomatically and decisively eased the mood within the rehearsal room, Simon would never suggest that behaving that way was a regular occurrence. "Losing one's temper is a very bad thing to do but I think if you get to know somebody very well then you're allowed to a couple of times. It's not great; though it does clear the air a little bit."

These sudden lurches of behaviour in the rehearsal room are indicative of the atmosphere of the play. They are suggested from within the heart of the text itself, like Othello's epileptic fit. Even then, drawing attention to these textual details can elicit responses that are unexpected. With Othello suffering from a debilitating disorder, Iago has the physical authority for the first time in the relationship. It is during these moments in the production that Iago whispered delicately into Othello's ear and tenderly stroked Othello's cheek.

Many read this as a revelatory new reading of Iago and his obsession with and for Othello, with *The Telegraph* suggesting that "a window is thrown open onto the play." This was viewed as the manifestation of a guilty sexual desire or a subconscious yearning for intimacy between them and caused audiences to call into question Iago's sexuality.

Sam would always say that he had no specific reading of Iago in mind when he started rehearsing; for him *Othello* is too complex and multi-dimensional a play to offer a single interpretation. However, this re-appraisal of Iago's sexuality is clearly not what Sam had intended. "Iago is heterosexual. I think he has a fascination with Othello which is not homosexual, but the fascination of a different race, a different physical type, a different mind, a different sexual drive. I don't think he's in love with Othello, but I think that weirdly, as he destroys him, as he comes closer to him both physically and emotionally and begins to understand how he ticks, it sort of turns him on. It's a power trip, and that can be very sexual. I think that's where it shades over occasionally into accusations of homo-eroticism. But I don't think it's a homosexual love affair."

There are undoubtedly some roles when Simon makes the decision that the character is homosexual, such as in Deborah Warner's production of *Julius Caesar* for the Barbican. "Cassius, in my performance, was obviously gay", he says wearily, "because of 'I am who I am' and his wife not being mentioned at all." The absence of Cassius' wife, like the absence of Iago's children, is another omission from the source material which is arguably an internal direction within the writing and represents Shakespeare's opinion of a character.

This returns to the idea of Simon's sense of his own identity and his suitability for casting in certain roles, particularly in those roles that are alpha males. "Those are tricky for me. When I did *Major Barbara* at the National Theatre, part of the excitement of accepting the role of Undershaft was that he was an alpha male. I was playing opposite

Paul Ready, who also isn't usually cast as an alpha male. There was this big confrontation at the end of the play and we were both just stood there in rehearsals saying 'What on Earth do we do?' and we started giving ground and Nick [Hytner, the director of *Major Barbara*] had to stop us and force us into this real stag fight. Iago is also an alpha male, but perhaps as we'd done *Richard III* together Sam didn't think that it was such a risk."

One unexpected risk occurred during the rehearsal for Desdemona's death scene. "I hate bad stage deaths," says Sam. "When someone dies, it takes a long time, particularly when they're suffocated. I think you have to feel the weight of the death, viscerally feel what it's like to kill someone. Also I wanted Desdemona to be someone who fought hard to stay alive. You can tell by the scene that precedes it, she does not want to die."

The first attempt at the scene took place about three weeks into rehearsal when the ensemble had continued to work through the play in Sam's company-based way of investigation, playing through the scenes in different formats and using different exercises. During the rehearsal, Sam gave Claire Skinner the instruction to "fight him as much as you can." Skinner was claustrophobic and in fighting Othello off during the suffocation, she induced a panic attack.

"It was very, very disturbing. I don't think anyone in the room knew if Claire was acting or not. It turned out she wasn't, but didn't want to stop because she wanted to know what it felt like. I felt terribly guilty about it – you don't want to put an actor's life in danger – but I knew she was intelligent enough to stop if she wanted to." What appeared on stage night after night throughout the tour was her recall of the events of the first rehearsal and the panic attack she suffered at the time. "One rehearsal cracked that scene. It is an incredibly sordid death and, yes, does de-romanticise it."

Following Desdemona's death and Emilia's disclosure of Iago's involvement, his declaration under arrest is succinct: "Demand me nothing. What you know, you know / From this time forth I never will speak word." This sort of climatic, vengeful malevolence prefigures Simon's exit as Malvolio in *Twelfth Night*. Simon's own final analysis of Iago is equally bleak. "I think he is the only true psychopath that Shakespeare created. I hit a period of depression getting involved with him. He really is quite disturbed."

Interestingly, Iago was one of the performances least reliant on the image-based approach. "Actually, thinking about it now, I would say that the most complete performances Simon has given for any production that I have directed him in are the ones least based on images: Iago, Vanya, Leontes, and Lopakhin to a degree." Unlike the MCC tie and gloves of Thersites, the walking stick and barking dogs of Richard III or the Mao-suited and bare-footed Ariel, Iago had to exist within a legitimate social and military hierarchy as a soldier.

In order to create this legitimate framework, Sam and designer Anthony Ward went away from the 'timeless' space of previous productions, where Roman swords could sit alongside study lamps, and placed *Othello* in a fixed, twentieth-century, historical context. The set retained the clean lines and open space of all of the other scenic environments, but the costumes needed to reflect a specific and precise period and place.

Even if there was a departure from timelessness and a rehearsal approach begun with images, the clash between sentimentality and vulgarity was still very much in evidence but this time on the subject of the time context itself. "Perhaps I'm giving myself too much credit," concedes Simon, "but the naturalistic setting was a mutually decided thing I think. I do remember a discussion with Sam about the design of the costumes. The set had already been decided upon at that stage. Sam was exploring the possibility of setting *Othello* during the Second World War and I suggested the 1950s because that's somehow less sentimental. It's more workaday."

Simon acknowledges that *Othello* holds an interesting place in Sam's repertoire as the most naturalistic production that he's done. "It's absolutely secure in time and place. I know I was very keen on it being late in the 50s because I thought there were too many associations with the 40s that were unnecessary. The 50s has a useful area of repression and decorum about it. People behaved in a particular way: the feeling of suburbia coming out of austerity. Sam saw *Othello* as a chamber piece and as a domestic piece."

Iago exists at the dark epicentre of this domestic space. Unlike Richard III, the Machiavellian villain who announces and evaluates his plot throughout each soliloquy, the emotional ferocity of Iago's sexual jealousy and loathing finds him hastily assembling and adjusting strategies as he seizes upon events and opportunities:

Let me see now:
To get his place, and to plume my will
In double knavery. How, how? (I.iii.386-388)

'Tis here, but yet confus'd:
Knavery's plain face is never seen till us'd. (II.ii.305-306)

Iago, then, is not one of the choric figures that offer a commentary upon an angle of a production, or offer clues into the director's interpretation of a play. "It's interesting to break them down into those sorts of categories," says Sam, offering an alternative approach to grouping the characters. For him, Richard III belongs to the set of characters that are certain of their realities at the beginning of the play, along with Ariel and Malvolio. "The journeys of those roles which are built slowly from the ground up are an easy process in some ways. Their realities then get destroyed on some level either gradually or suddenly."

On the other end of the scale are those roles where you have to launch into a state of crisis with a completely distorted environment right from the beginning of the play such as Leontes and Vanya. "They are the difficult ones where you have to bring a whole lifetime, a whole marriage, a whole set of relationships on stage with you." Iago lies in the middle of the spectrum. "Those in the middle, in a sense, are Simon's most complete performances, at least for me: particularly Thersites and Iago. Iago does not start in a state of crisis."

That said, this was still not a role that you could creep up on gradually and required an enormous amount of preparation prior to each and every performance. "Simon was in character for hours before he went on stage; he was getting into the skin. It's the only time that I've walked into his dressing room before a show and he'd be sitting there completely still and silent surrounded by a very dark aura. I wouldn't really want to have a conversation with him. He didn't want to talk. He wasn't unpleasant; he just didn't want to say anything. He'd just be sitting there smoking. Iago is a gift of a role in many ways but this growing malice of the man was fully realised. He really went there with Iago and I thought that it produced a superlative performance."

In addition to the naturalism of the production, *Othello* is unique in their joint repertoire in many ways. Their first three productions happened within four years during the early nineties at the RSC. There is a four year interim between the last of these productions, *The*

Tempest, and *Othello* in 1997, marking the first occasion where their neat relationship was picked up again in a new rehearsal room. Sam was midway through his tenure as the Artistic Director of the Donmar Warehouse, whilst Simon was enjoying new success in productions of *Rosencrantz and Guildenstern are Dead* and *Volpone* at the National Theatre, then under the directorship of Richard Eyre.

"I'd managed to wheedle my way into the National – it wasn't easy I tell you. I'd auditioned for them before. Both the RSC and the National didn't want me the first time around. Anyway, I was there but I don't think that the fact I was at the National particularly effected where we did our next production. Richard Eyre is a great fan of Sam's and Sam is a great fan of Richard. Then *Othello* was on the cards."

As well as being a fan of Richard Eyre's, Sam was also an enthusiast for the work of the great German director Peter Stein and, similarly, the appreciation was mutual. *Othello* originated as a co-production between the National Theatre and the Salzburg Festival, then under the artistic directorship of Stein. When Stein finally saw the production and the rigid, naturalistic, twentieth-century imaginative universe that had been created, he remarked in a subsequent platform discussion that Sam's was a very "retro" production. "Retro-chic," Sam shot back swiftly.

Indeed Stein couldn't understand how sticking to the meter could be liberating or why Mendes' setting was 'modern.' Sam is equally self-critical. "We're obsessed in Britain with heritage. Shakespeare is one of the few things that makes us feel secure and successful."

The co-production was to preview in the Cottesloe auditorium of the National Theatre before playing dates at the Salzburg Festival, then returning to the Cottesloe for its official Press Night and initial run. Following the appearances for both co-producers, the production would then embark on an international tour. and would ultimately end up back at the National Theatre, though this time in the larger auditorium of the Lyttelton.

This would be the first occasion when their work would be seen outside the UK, though their work had toured previously. In a similar scenario to the Cottesloe – tour – Lyttelton arrangement, *Richard III* had begun at The Other Place then toured nationally before returning to the RSC in the larger auditorium of The Swan.

Simon acknowledges that in terms of process of putting together a production the distinction between the two largest theatre companies in the UK is minimal. "When you're in a rehearsal room there's not much difference between working at the RSC or the NT."

Another departure was in Sam's decision to cast an Othello who was significantly younger than usual. He was keen that the difficulty within the relationship shouldn't be based on the dynamic of an older man and a younger woman.

Originally, the role was to go to Adrian Lester who had just won an Olivier Award for *Company* at the Donmar Warehouse which Sam had directed. He was no stranger to Shakespeare either, having received an Olivier Award nomination for his portrayal of Rosalind in Cheek By Jowl's all-male version of *As You Like It.* Not long after accepting the role, Adrian received an offer for one of the lead roles in a new film called *Primary Colors* to be directed by Mike Nichols and starring John Travolta, Emma Thompson and Kathy Bates amongst other Hollywood heavyweights.

"It was a very funny conversation when Sam phoned up and I think he had Richard Eyre and possibly Trevor Nunn with him. He said he was phoning from the National and there was bad news and that Adrian had dropped out. What?! Why?! He's been offered a big film in Hollywood. Oh, fine, fair enough. He's got plenty of time to do Othello. It wasn't that late into the process; I think that Claire [Skinner, playing Desdemona] and I were the only two other people cast. Sam moved fairly quickly to get David [Harewood]."

Like Adrian Lester, David Harewood was born in Birmingham, had graduated from RADA and was enjoying a successful career, but his work was largely unknown to London audiences. Equally, he was no stranger to Shakespeare, having played Edmund in *King Lear* for Talawa and Antony opposite Vanessa Redgrave's Cleopatra at the Public Theater in New York.

For Sam, when casting David Harewood, or Adrian Lester before him, the age of the role was secondary to the breadth of inspiration and depth that any actor would need to bring to the role. "I depend a great deal, as any director does, on the imagination of their actors. You bring in and cast somebody who you know is the right age and the right type but also the right imagination and the right level of spiritual understanding."

In boldly choosing to cast a younger actor, Sam was not prepared to let the shadow of previous performances of this famous play affect his decision-making process, though he does confess that fear is sometimes unavoidable. With *Richard III* "Tony Sher's spider-like shadow hung over the whole affair to a degree, compared to *Troilus and Cressida* with a less domineering personality."

One of the hallmarks of *Othello*'s long production history is the reported antagonism between the actors portraying Othello and Iago. "David and I were very keen that we as actors should not be rivals. We were both very keen that it should not be unpleasant between us as actors. That was an absolute imperative thing right from the beginning. I'd read so many things about Iagos and Othellos not getting on, and so had he, and I hate all of that sort of thing. It doesn't interest me particularly."

Instead, Simon had nothing but praise for his counterpart. "I didn't know David's acting before at all but he was magnificent, at top speed, when he was really on form, those last moments were just heartbreaking."

Although this production may have been a point of departure in many ways – a transition from the RSC to the NT, a naturalistic rather than timeless setting, a move away from an image-based rehearsal process – some hallmarks of the collaborations are still apparent.

Iago is the first of Simon's 'lonely men working at a desk.' "I wanted him to be a pen pusher. I didn't want him to be an active soldier. Iago had a couple of desk moments. It was in a scene where I had a soliloquy at a desk, and it's not even his desk, it's the Duke's desk. The desk is a recurring motif, but I'm very fond of inappropriate briefcases too, especially briefcases that don't quite fit the person, because briefcases are ugly things, I think. Iago was this lumpy man, in a uniform that doesn't quite fit, with his briefcase, and it just smells of failure."

In many ways Shakespeare, Sam and Simon have done their upmost to highlight Iago's powerlessness: the childless marriage possibly stemming from his impotence, his lack of advancement, and the sense of him as a workmanlike pencil-pusher.

IAGO He holds me well.
The better shall my purpose work on him.
Cassio's a proper man. Let me see now:
To get his place, and to plume up my will
In double knavery. How, how? Let' see.
After some time to abuse Othello's ear
That he is too familiar with his wife.
He hath a person and a smooth dispose

To be suspected – fram'd to make women false
The Moor is of a free and open nature
That thinks men honest that but seem to be so,
And will as tenderly be led by th'nose
As asses are. [I.iii.384-396]

During the soliloquy, Iago remained seated at a desk (not even his own) mapping out the fragments of his confused mind using a deck of playing cards to represent each of the characters he mentions. Using an innocent pastime to coordinate his malevolent schemes reminded *The Guardian*'s Michael Billington of WH Auden's description of Iago as the joker in the pack.

Simon's approach to Iago's accent was similar to his approach to Lopakhin's accent a few years later, another of the characters not based on images and in the middle of Sam's spectrum of those characters that begin in certainty or begin in crisis. "I was quite keen that Iago should be low class, partly because I'm crap at accents. I was interested in this British military outpost feel. I love the pettiness of that, or that representation of pettiness, and the whole world fitted that little small-mindedness."

One of Sam's predominant concerns when creating a production to tour is that the show is robust enough to withstand the demands of travelling to different venues over a lengthy course of time. "When you're building something to last eleven months and it has to tour the world, you'd better build it properly. You don't want to get an actor who a month into the run suddenly thinks 'we never explored the idea of...' Then it collapses like a house of cards. They're right to explore and it is interesting but it topples everything if people don't have the time to work out what it means for their character and how they might respond. You can't throw that into the middle of a run."

Othello then was a departure into a new ensemble-based approach of having the full company present for all rehearsals and conducting sessions of 'three dimensional literary criticism' in exploring a scene from a multitude of perspectives and angles. This ensures that there is an opportunity to try a number of approaches and motivations and doesn't leave the lingering and potentially detrimental feeling that there is an unexplored avenue that may have produced a better end result if only the time constraints of rehearsals had allowed.

"I remember obsessively working on the first scene between Iago and Roderigo having Simon and Crispin walking around the circle of the space playing the scene over and over again. Iago trotting after Roderigo and now Roderigo trotting after Iago and now the two walking in parallel and then the two walking and stopping and then Roderigo walking back and forth and Iago still, then the other way around. I was trying to unlock the level of Iago's pretence and how far we should be aware, at the beginning of the play, of his lie and how good he was and how much, therefore he improved as liar over the course of the play. Everything at that point seemed to be the first two scenes of the play: Iago and Roderigo and Othello's first appearance. We just banged on and on; we must have done it for four days."

During these various set-ups rehearsing the early scenes of *Othello*, the actors were not constrained to playing their own characters. Simon would play Roderigo and Crispin Letts would play Iago. On other occasions, Simon or Claire Skinner would portray Othello and David Harewood would portray Iago or Desdemona. "We had a great day where I thought that Claire was getting extremely bored and frustrated being murdered by Othello over and over again, so she played Othello for a day and David was murdered over and over again, which was good for him to be the person who experienced being suffocated."

"As a young director one of the reasons why I was successful at a young age was that I have a facility for staging. Organising action wasn't difficult for me. It wasn't always good but it was always passable. It was fair to say that I could stage most scenes in an hour. If you want me to stage it I can stage it and it might even feel good for a couple of days. But you won't have explored it properly, and problems will open up. Now I think that these things need to be built properly. Built to last."

This was a process that started during the *Othello* rehearsals and was developed and refined during *Uncle Vanya* and *Twelfth Night* which transferred from the Donmar Warehouse to the Brooklyn Academy of Music and *The Winter's Tale* and *The Cherry Orchard* which were also being designed for a lengthy, international tour as part of the first phase of The Bridge Project.

UNCLE VANYA

"It's worth taking the risk and pushing it to the extreme"

UNCLE VANYA by ANTON CHEKHOV
In a new version by BRIAN FRIEL
FIRST PERFORMANCE: Donmar Warehouse, London, 6 September 2002
SUBSEQUENT PERFORMANCES:
Brooklyn Academy of Music, New York, 10 January – 9 March 2003

CAST

SIMON RUSSELL BEALE	Vanya
DAVID BRADLEY	Serebryakov
SELINA CADELL	Maria
LUKE JARDINE	Yefim
HELEN McCRORY	Yelena
CHERRY MORRIS	Marina
ANTHONY O'DONNELL	Ilya Telegin
GYURI SAROSSY	Petrushka
MARK STRONG	Astrov
EMILY WATSON	Sonya

CREATIVE TEAM

SAM MENDES	Director
ANTHONY WARD	Set Designer
MARK THOMPSON	Costume Designer
HUGH VANSTONE	Lighting
GEORGE STILES	Music
PAUL ARDITTI	Sound

"I have measured out my life in Uncle Vanyas from Olivier's legendary Chichester production to Peter Stein's luminous Italian version. But Sam Mendes's revival, with its mixture of visual clarity and emotional charity, unquestionably belongs in the premier league ... Mendes's cast capture brilliantly the characters' journey from ignorance to knowledge in the course of a disruptive summer. Simon Russell Beale's Vanya is simply amazing. He offers you the spectacle of an ironic, intelligent 47-year-old man gazing at Yelena with the dotty helplessness of a moonstruck adolescent: aware of his own absurdity but powerless to prevent it. But Russell Beale is at his finest in the great scene where he wakes from his dream at the news that the professor plans to sell the estate: he seethes with impotent fury at the realisation that his self-denying existence has been totally without point. And, as he denies the professor's charge that he is a 'nonentity', Rusell Beale extends a charity to the character that beautifully matches Chekhov's. What Mendes conveys, however, is the extent to which all the characters' lives have been changed in the course of a summer. Crowning an excellent evening is Anthony Ward's design. But the ultimate test of any Vanya *is whether it stirs you to the depths of your soul; and that is one which Mendes's production passes with flying colours."*

(Michael Billington, *Guardian*, 18 September 2002)

After twelve years of collaboration and four productions of Shakespeare plays this was the first show that Simon and Sam worked on together by another playwright. Just as when they embarked on *Troilus and Cressida* they had each only worked on one previous Shakespeare play, so they had each been involved in one other Chekhov prior to *Uncle Vanya*: for Sam it was *The Cherry Orchard* in the West End and Simon had played Konstantin in *The Seagull* at the RSC in the same season as Thersites.

"The idea of doing a Chekhov together was interesting. I've always wanted to do a modern play with Sam but we've never got around to it. It's not completely arbitrary that we've ended up doing so much Shakespeare but it wasn't a positive decision on either of our parts, it's just worked out that way. Sam wasn't against the idea of me doing parts other than Shakespeare, what an appalling idea! I'd had such a wonderful experience doing *The Seagull*. Yet *Uncle Vanya* was so very exciting. I loved that production. I absolutely loved it."

In some respects, fresh translations can seem like new contemporary plays. Unlike the process for *The Cherry Orchard*, the adaptor wasn't present in rehearsals so the company didn't refer to an original or literal translation throughout the rehearsal process. "It didn't cross my mind as to whether Brian Friel's translation was a classic play or modern play. By and large you don't ever think 'Oh, gosh, we're doing a great classical play.' Actually, that's not entirely true. There always comes that moment of 'Oh, shit, I'm doing Hamlet,' but for the most part in the rehearsal room you don't think like that."

The work of the rehearsal room consisted of the "high pitch" at which Vanya begins the play and pushing Simon towards this. On his first appearance in Act I, Vanya has been asleep inside the house fully clothed in the middle of the day and emerges looking "rumpled." "I was determined for him not to wander on looking all tousled and teddy-bear lovable and gradually sidle up to the part because I don't think that's how it's written. When you start with Vanya, he's already at a certain emotional pitch and Simon was trying to creep into it sideways, to get in through the back door if you like, and I wanted him to come bursting out of the front door."

"I remember saying to him, 'The play's called *Uncle Vanya*, you've got to come on like you're Uncle Vanya, stop creeping on like you're a stage hand in the darkness. Why are you not coming out of the house in a state of emotional turmoil?" Vanya is incapable of thinking of anything except that Yelena lives in the same house and that he is desperately in love with her. He hates her husband Serebryakov and he literally can't sleep to the extent at which he's sleeping at unconventional hours of the day. "You come out on a fever pitch. He's on the edge. You can't tiptoe up to it."

"It's that slightly expositional beginning which happens with Chekhov. By the time you get to *The Cherry Orchard* it's virtually disappeared but it's still there with *Uncle Vanya*: waking up, coming onto stage and giving you the story of his life." It was this aspect of the start of the play that Simon was having trouble with and none of the various set-ups explored in the rehearsal room – playing the piano or eating for example – were providing Simon with the necessary state of release.

Sam was continually reinforcing that Simon should just trust the material. "I kept telling Sam that I was at a complete loss and in a last desperate attempt I said 'It's the writing.' He said 'Don't blame the writing, it is brilliant writing, now just get on with it,' which is quite right. Anyway, I got terribly angry."

"During the third or fourth preview we were in the Green Room and I said 'I don't know what the fuck you're doing in the first scene,'" confesses Sam. "Which is very unlike me, I'm very non-confrontational. It was partly that I felt he needed a kick but it wasn't entirely strategic; it was emotional. I was frustrated. 'I've given you this note three times now. You're missing the first act. You're playing catch up until the middle of Act II.'"

It is absolutely understandable that two creative individuals who are both passionate and committed to producing the highest quality standard of work would have disagreements, especially over the course of a twenty year relationship when you know each other well and your collaboration is built upon challenging each other to achieve your best. Simon and Sam are no exception.

The difficulties with the first act of *Uncle Vanya* did provide the occasion of what Simon describes as "the funniest of our disagreements," during one of the preview performances. "I think Kate [Winslet] had seen one of the shows and said 'Why doesn't he just sit down and tell his story? Which I remember I thought I should do in the first place, but that's another story and I'm sure that Sam would tell a totally different version! Anyway, we were rowing about this and eventually Vanya did just sit down. I went on that evening very angry and so consequently that first scene had a sort of outright power behind it."

This was achieving the desired effect of having Vanya begin the play at a high pitch. "Sam was sat out in the audience thinking 'Good old Simon, well done, he's getting over the loss of temper and he's doing exactly what I asked him to do.' I was supposed to move a little during the scene and I didn't. Sam was thinking 'Why isn't he moving there? For goodness sake I've just given him these notes.' Anyway, when I got up from the table it became clear that the laces of the old fashioned boots I was wearing had become completely tied together and I actually couldn't move my feet. The reason I was completely still was because I couldn't move at all. And there had been Sam sat in the audience seething!"

Sam believes that one of the best moments in his production of *Uncle Vanya* was the entrance of Yelena and it represents another example of pushing ideas to their maximum point. As written, "SEREBRYAKOV, YELENA, SONYA *and* TELEGIN *enter*" together, having just returned from a walk. As directed by Sam, Serebryakov and Telegin entered, crossed the stage and exited. Yelena came on to stage on her own in total silence, watched by both Astrov and Vanya; she very slowly crossed the stage on her own; she poured a glass of tea; she drank it and she exited. "And nothing was said. Yet in that pause the whole play is laid out before you: Yelena as a sexual mischief maker or as an innocent; Vanya and Astrov both as people who have either fallen in love or are about to fall in love with her and whose futures will be changed because of that. It's all there, but it's one half line of stage direction. It's a question of how you unlock those little moments. It's worth taking the risk and pushing it to the extreme."

Vanya's drunken declaration of love for Yelena in Act II was also pushed to its maximum point. The only stage directions here are "*She attempts to go. He blocks her*," and "*He grabs her hand and kisses it.*" Yet in the production Vanya was crawling on his knees towards, literally kissing her garment. This was one of the reasons why Vanya had to begin the play in a state of emotional turmoil; otherwise this moment would seem incongruous in the character's overall arc. "It's a wonderful scene, but if Act I isn't right, you're not ready for it, it seems forced."

The family scene of Act III was another example of the blank canvas way of working with multiple set-ups, including one with Simon lying prostrate across the dining table. "I remember Sam working very hard on the third act of Vanya – that family scene with the very long table and the idea that you don't set anything at all. At all."

Vanya, like Leontes in *The Winter's Tale*, requires of the actor an emotional jump. For both these characters, Simon found that the jump manifested itself as a howl of pain. For Leontes, it was in the scene where Paulina tells him Hermione is dead. For Vanya, the moment is in Act III, when Serebryakov tells him that the estate that he has loyally worked on is going to be sold. Vanya attacks him:

VANYA	I worked like an ox for ten years until the bank loan was paid off –
SEREBRYAKOV	Why did I ever start this?
VANYA	– with the result that the estate is now free of debt and in good shape and all because I worked myself to the bone and now in my old age I'm to be kicked out on the roadside. Wonderful!
SEREBRYAKOV	Nobody is going to kick you –
VANYA	For twenty-five years I've run this place more faithfully than any manager; and for twenty-five years money was sent to him every month; and for twenty-five years I earned the same princely salary, five hundred roubles. Never one rouble more. Never an offer of one rouble more. For twenty-five years never even a Thank You, for God's sake!

(*Uncle Vanya*, Act III)

"It was like mallet hits – twenty five years, twenty five years, twenty five years. A lot of work up until then was about holding back. You don't want to splash too early, there's a knack to it, but on that particular day I remember I just decided to go for it. It's the result of twenty five years of frustration. This moment came after a long period of Sam just pushing and pushing and pushing and pushing and I've seen him do it with other actors as well. He's very good at that. He'll wait until it pops."

Sometimes the downside of making a breakthrough to that level of emotional intensity can be that it is difficult to rediscover on a nightly basis. This is true for the howls of pain that Simon found for Vanya and, later, Leontes. "I don't know where it came from and I didn't locate it quickly enough. I've never quite been able to recreate it."

As with *The Cherry Orchard*, Act IV is a point of departure as Serebryakov and Yelena are leaving for the last time. During their final parting "Before she left, Vanya abased himself before Yelena as if he had nothing else to lose and he was literally grovelling on the ground at her feet. Horrible, horrible," remembers Simon. "Vanya broke my heart. He absolutely broke my heart." He finishes the play as another "lonely man working at his desk," as the everyday drudgery and monotony of his existence falls back into its routine.

TWELFTH NIGHT

"I wish we'd kept the humbugs"

TWELFTH NIGHT by WILLIAM SHAKESPEARE
FIRST PERFORMANCE: Donmar Warehouse, London, 11 October 2002
SUBSEQUENT PERFORMANCES:
Brooklyn Academy of Music, New York, 10 January – 9 March 2003

CAST

SIMON RUSSELL BEALE	Malvolio
DAVID BRADLEY	Andrew Aguecheek
SELINA CADELL	Maria
LUKE JARDINE	Fabian
PAUL JESSON	Toby Belch
HELEN McCRORY	Olivia
CHERRY MORRIS	Lady
ANTHONY O'DONNELL	Feste
GARY POWELL	Antonio
GYURI SAROSSY	Sebastian
MARK STRONG	Orsino
EMILY WATSON	Viola

CREATIVE TEAM

SAM MENDES	Director
ANTHONY WARD	Set Designer
MARK THOMPSON	Costume Designer
HUGH VANSTONE	Lighting
GEORGE STILES	Music
PAUL ARDITTI	Sound

"BAM, through March 9, is hosting the exclusive US engagement of Sam Mendes's London productions of Uncle Vanya *and* Twelfth Night, *his farewell, after 10 years, as artistic director of the 250-seat Donmar Warehouse. Donmar's reputation for daring – and effective – theater far exceeds its diminutive size. And Mr. Mendes's own reputation could not be higher at the moment, thanks to his direction of the films American Beauty and Road to Perdition... [T]he richest fare was onstage, where Mr. Mendes links two plays 'about requited and unrequited love, by two of the greatest playwrights that ever lived' with a supertitle – 'O learn to read what silent love hath write' from Shakespeare's 'Sonnet 23' – and clever cross casting: acclaimed stage actor Simon Russell Beale, for example, plays both Vanya and Malvolio. [...] He is already being called one of the best actors of his generation and heir to the crown now worn by Michael Gambon. [...] Above all Mr. Russell Beale's Malvolio, Olivia's preening, self-important, Bible-reading servant, who now wears a hairnet and dreams, on a simple cot, of a life of wealth and ease with his beautiful employer. Messrs. Mendes and Russell Beale credit Malvolio with a flawed but no less palpable humanity, which makes the cruel hoax visited upon him far more painful to watch than the similar real-life stunt of Joe Millionaire."*

(B.D. Phillips, *Wall Street Journal*, 21 January 2003)

Following the casting, Sam and Simon rarely have preliminary meetings. Simon likes to be left to consider the character rather than have a responsibility for the overall production and, unless a specific design idea affected the character Simon was playing, which may make him prepare for the character differently, Sam does not interrupt those thoughts. "I don't want to burden him with what the production may be or may not be. Anyway, I'm a big one for changing my mind so I don't tend to make announcements or pronouncements before I start about what the design will be. I let it emerge."

Perhaps the process of collaborating has made preliminary meetings redundant as they are now on a similar wavelength about the design world of any play. "I know what Simon likes and I do think about him when I'm working with the designer. There is a sense when he looks at the sets or the clothes or whatever and he'll go 'Oh, yes, I see.' He doesn't get involved in the design world, although we always have chats and he trusts me to get on with it. He knows that it's going to be quite a simple canvas always, just of a different sort."

"He's not a looker-over-my-shoulder, of which there are many. There are certain actors that really do want to know: What are you going to do? How is it going to be? What's the world? They are looking for guidance from externals which I'm not willing to give. You should never really give advice from externals. It shouldn't matter what clothes you're wearing in the first three of four weeks of rehearsals because apart from anything else you haven't decided who the characters are yet." This suggests that Sam very much favours the idea of working from 'the inside out,' and establishing the interior emotional life of the characters prior to exploring how they interact with the set and what they're wearing. The one example from their collaboration of working from 'the outside in,' would be Ariel, when the initial parameters of the character's emotional landscape were unclear.

In fact, across their eight current collaborations their only preliminary meeting has been for *Twelfth Night*. "I think Sam would, out of interest, phone and say I've got so and so for casting, but that's just a bit of fun really. I've got no more involvement than that, deliberately, because I'm a crap caster and anyway it's not my job. Occasionally, if he's really stuck he'll phone to discuss ideas about something but it's very rare. More often he's giving me an idea."

That was certainly the case for the preliminary meeting for *Twelfth Night*, which took place in a small cafe in Covent Garden. "I don't remember why we were meeting particularly. I can't really remember having preliminary meetings about shows with Sam at all but I can't think why we'd have just met for a drink," says Simon alluding to their 'neat' relationship. "Perhaps it was a general throwing around of ideas." This was where Sam suggested the idea of the letter scene taking place in Malvolio's bedroom, which was definitely a design idea that directly affected how Simon would start thinking about the character. "What would happen if the letter was read in bed, if we were given access to Malvolio's private space?"

In the text of *Twelfth Night* the letter scene takes place in the garden of the Countess Olivia's residence. Maria has forged her mistress' handwriting and created a cryptic letter as a way of gulling the puritanical Malvolio into believing that Olivia is in love with him and that his status is to be elevated. Sir Toby, Sir Andrew and Fabian hide in a box tree to see the effects of the letter and the comic misunderstandings ensue.

This delicately placed idea provided a springboard of further inspiration for Simon, who rushed back to Sam after the meeting had finished with a series of further thoughts: what if he's caught swigging from a bottle of vodka? Or eating humbugs? Or looking at a pornographic magazine?

The long-standing joke between Sam and Simon that one of them is a classicist with a vulgar streak and the other is a vulgarian with a classical streak has continued for so long that neither of them can remember who was originally which; that at various times throughout their association they have each been both, but never at the same time. They always complement one another: one is always the classicist and one is always the vulgarian. "It's a balance of pushing things a bit too far and somebody pulling you back on both sides."

In this case, it was Sam that needed to rein Simon in a little. The ideas of the vodka and the pornography were dismissed almost instantaneously as both agreed that, whatever Malvolio may be, he certainly isn't a hypocrite. The idea of humbugs as a sort of guilty pleasure indulged in a private space lasted further into the rehearsals and was eventually dropped. Yet, the placement of the initial idea had begun the process of discovering various opportunities and avenues within the character.

"That is a technique that Sam uses on me: he occasionally has an idea that provokes something and I know he's aware of what happens to me because he's mentioned it. I'll suddenly see him light up with an idea. That's sometimes a tactic he uses with me. That induces six or seven steps to produce humbugs but more importantly to produce a sense of arrested development in Malvolio – repression and single beds – and that leads on to all sorts of associations and ideas. Sam loves that possibility of placing an idea."

Sam is certainly aware of what happens to Simon when such an idea is placed. "It's like suddenly providing the string onto which the pearls are going to be strung. Simon has a very unusual mixture of exceptional intelligence and high, high-level textual analysis and the actor's show-off instinct. How would that read to an audience? He's very, very aware of an audience, even if he pretends not to be as it's sometimes undignified for a classical actor to say that. He's immensely in touch with that side of things. Joking aside, when we talk about being classicists with vulgar streaks, I think what he means by 'vulgar' is 'with an acute sense of the audience.' It's a combination of things. It matches very much my own favoured way of working which is to be acutely aware of the text and then at times to play fast and loose and take an idea and stretch it to its maximum point."

The process of being aware of the text but stretching new ideas almost to breaking point is not a new approach. Although these plays have maintained their popularity for over four hundred years, it is essential that each new production engages with the contemporary audience of its time, in the same way that the original texts offered a commentary of Elizabethan and Jacobean England even if the events depicted were historical. It is a requirement of each new generation of productions to offer a fresh interpretation, and often strong visual ideas provide the means by which productions are discussed, be it Peter Brook's white-box *A Midsummer Night's Dream* or Rupert Goold's arctic wasteland *The Tempest*. In many ways, this production of *Twelfth Night* is referred to be 'the bedroom scene' rather than 'the letter scene.'

Whilst he acknowledges a certain joy in knowing that you're presenting an audience with something they definitely won't have seen before, Simon is also clear that it isn't a process of self-congratulatory reinvention. "It's a dangerous game to play that. The second reaction to that is 'Oh, Jesus, why can't they do it in the garden where Shakespeare has set it.' I'm sure there is a delight in it but it's more important than that: it's about Malvolio's inner life. Of course, setting the scene in the garden would have done that as well – Shakespeare's no fool – but the bedroom sort of pushed that idea even further. It's voyeuristic. It's like seeing someone on the loo. You're not supposed to see Malvolio in his bedroom."

Whether there is an official preliminary meeting or not, there is always the opportunity to drop in an idea, even if it's just over the telephone and inevitably, some of the ideas will be followed through to the realised production, as with the bedroom scene, and some ideas will be abandoned as other choices are made throughout the rehearsals. "Sometimes I make those suggestions early on, knowing that they'll have a domino effect and sometimes they'll lead nowhere. I was convinced I was saying something interesting to Simon about Leontes when I said Leontes is incapable of sleep; we talked for a while about insomnia. I was convinced I was going to start the production of *The Winter's Tale* with this man alone in this place unable to sleep. It was an idea that we both thought was fascinating to begin with and it got completely disinteresting by the first week of rehearsals. Sometimes you think you have a few clues and it turns out that it's not worth pursuing."

Arguably the most ensemble play in Shakespeare's canon, *Twelfth Night*, features a gallery of memorable characters including the frequently soused knights Sir Toby Belch and Sir Andrew Aguecheek, the wise fool Feste and the 'gull catching' gentlewoman Maria. The main thrust of the story deals with two twins, Viola and Sebastian, separated by a shipwreck and stranded on the coast of Illyria, each believing that the other is dead. Viola disguises herself as a boy to serve in the court of Duke Orsino and is assigned to woo the Countess Olivia on his behalf. Viola has fallen desperately in love with Orsino but follows his instructions, only for Olivia to fall in love with Viola's male alter ego. The mistaken identity provides both a serious sexual conundrum and a series of comedic confusions.

Yet the role that has come to define the production is Malvolio, with King Charles I's Master of the Revels recording the play neither as *Twelfth Night* nor by its subtitle *What You Will* but simply as *Malvolio*. This may be surprising given the size of the role. It led Maddy Costa to question in an article in *The Guardian* "What do they see in Malvolio? On paper, there is little to recommend him: he is unforgiving and rude; he criticises his mistress, Olivia, while massaging his rampant ego with indulgent dreams of life as her husband. His austerity is born of a Puritanism that makes him intolerant of revelry." Yet Simon was the first of a series of recent high-profile turns in the part that include Patrick Stewart at Chichester, Derek Jacobi for the Donmar in the West End and Richard Wilson for the RSC in Stratford and in London.

For Michael Boyd, Artistic Director of the RSC, it is not a 'leading role', but it is what he calls an 'opportunity role'. "Malvolio is clearly at odds with the world, and possibly with himself: that kind of internal drama is always tasty for an actor. Plus, he has these two amazing set pieces that are practically announced by the other characters – 'Wait till you see this!'" Michael Grandage, who succeeded Sam as the Artistic Director of the Donmar Warehouse, agrees about the conflict within Malvolio, and also the breadth of his storyline. "Malvolio follows a particular arc. He is utterly pompous at the beginning, then gives himself over to love and lets an audience enjoy how foolish he looks. Then he is incarcerated, and goes to a really profound place because of that."

Certainly in his first two appearances he has little to do other than respond to Olivia's particular whims. In Act I, Scene 5 he chastises Feste who has been long absent from the household and is then sent on an errand to give Cesario – Viola's alter ego – a ring which in Act II, Scene 1 we see him complete with brusque efficiency. "He's a functionary. He might be a very rude functionary, but that's all he is at this point, we haven't really gotten to know him at all. In fact, that's not true because we know that he's rude and a bit of a bully, but that's about it," says Simon.

During Act II, Scene 3, the two knights Sir Toby Belch and Sir Andrew Aguecheek return to Olivia's house in the middle of the night in a drunken stupor and having just indulged in a large meal. In this production, this left them incredibly flatulent and, with the assistance of an off-stage 'fart machine', the actors punctuated the proceedings by breaking wind:

SIR TOBY Does not our lives consist of the four elements? [Fart]

SIR ANDREW Faith, so they say; but I think it rather consists of eating and drinking. [Fart]

SIR TOBY Thou'rt a scholar. [Fart]

(II.iii.9-12)

"The audience loved it. It brought the house down, predictably when you've got David Bradley (Aguecheek) and Paul Jesson (Belch)," says Sam proudly. "I've got the sense of humour of a pre-pubescent boy. I have absolutely no humiliation," he confesses. Simon also recalls that this mischievous sense of humour was also at work in the rehearsal room: "The fart machine in *Twelfth Night*! Oh, dear. Occasionally he would just use it at random in a perfectly ordinary scene or even in serious rehearsals and Lucy our stage manager got embarrassed so easily and used to blush every time. It's terrible! It's so childish!"

Clearly another idea that registers on the spectrum of vulgarity versus classicism, Sam is quick to come to his own defence. "I hate the line that says that Shakespeare didn't have a vulgar sense of humour. It's there constantly in all of the plays. Some of the worst fart and willy gags that you've seen on the professional stage are in Shakespeare's plays. People were surprised by the dance in *The Winter's Tale* but it's the dance of satyrs, it's a rite of spring, it's a 'sex dance'. It's in the text! I do have a silly sense of humour but at the same time I wouldn't put the humour in incessantly if I didn't think it was helping an understanding of a character or a scene."

In the events on stage, Belch and Aguecheek are joined by Olivia's fool Feste and they continue their reverie with a catch song. They are interrupted firstly by Maria who rightly suspects that the steward Malvolio will not be far behind her. The text suggests that Olivia has been roused by the song and dispatched Malvolio to put an end to the disturbance. In this production, Simon entered as Malvolio in a hairnet: It was a small suggestion that "somehow, this lonely man does have a world that he inhabits somewhere off stage and that he's not just a functionary."

The hairnet was also indicative of a man who was constantly preening himself as a way of claiming a certain amount of status. It covered his fastidiously slicked-back hair. He walked in a sort of officious mince with a ramrod-straight back. Everything on the surface denoted a studied priggishness, but beneath the character's affectations, lurked the fascination of the character's interior life.

The phrase 'lonely man' is indicative of Simon's feeling of compassion and empathy towards Malvolio. "I know it's a sentimental reading of him but he's by himself. He's got no support mechanism anywhere. What does he do in the evenings? Read a book? Listen to Radio 2? Actually that's a wonderful idea: easy listening radio, that would have been marvellous! But we can't go back." These clues to Malvolio's inner life stem right back to the preliminary meeting where both Sam and Simon were searching for clues into what this puritanical man does in his own time to seek solace and, crucially, comfort. "Sam turned around recently and said, I think jokingly, 'I wish we'd kept the humbugs.' Obviously the vodka and the pornography are wrong because he's not a hypocrite but the humbugs... I don't know. There's just something about comfort."

With the decision taken that the famous Act II, Scene 5 letter scene was to take place in Malvolio's bedroom, there was another window into the private existence that Malvolio inhabited. The sense of freedom, possibility and comfort that the character feels in that scene also extends to the actor. "It's interesting that is the scene I enjoyed most in terms of release. I felt released and the idea fitted."

Conversely, Simon didn't feel the same enjoyment with Malvolio's next appearance. Buoyed on by the encouragement in Maria's letter which he supposes is from Olivia, Malvolio doggedly follows every instruction. Upon his next entrance in Act III, Scene 4, he appears dressed in cross gartered yellow stockings with a persistent smile. He is also seen kissing his hand repeatedly, much to the confusion of Olivia and the hidden delight of Maria. Not only is the scene one of the most famous in the play, it is also a comedic high point for the audience.

Simon never felt comfortable playing that scene and still has many doubts about it retrospectively. "Malvolio is not an idiot, so to dress up idiotically, even in the madness of love, seems unlikely. I've read various ideas about what cross-gartering is; cross-gartering and yellow stockings is not a ludicrous idea but it seems a very old fashioned idea, it's sort of plus-fours. I'm still confused about that scene – what does the smile mean? I think for a modern audience we're sort of stuck with that scene in a sort of nowhere house."

As such, he argues, it becomes necessary to find a suitable code that translates what is happening in the text to the contemporary understanding of the modern audience. "We did have to find a code, but it was one that didn't quite correspond to me to what Malvolio is trying to do. I had real problems with the code that was used for Malvolio's costume, especially with the yellow stockings. I think I ended up with yellow socks with slight cross hatching but it didn't quite work. Looking back on it, I only had this thought later after we'd stopped doing it, but I wondered whether we couldn't have found a different idea or gone in a different direction. I found that scene very uncomfortable and I never quite settled down. I never quite sorted that one out."

It is clear that Simon's sense of failure about this scene, even with Sam's encouragement to the contrary, is still palpable. Equally, there is an apparent correlation between Simon searching for 'comfort' for Malvolio the isolated character and the actor looking for 'release' to have the freedom to play within the scene. Whereas in the letter scene, Simon felt released by the idea of transposing the scene to the bedroom and was able to play and enjoy the scene, the code adopted for the yellow stockings scene was constrictive and trapping. "I didn't feel released in that scene which is why I feel I failed at it."

It remains to this day the role on which they've collaborated that Simon doesn't feel he fully realised. "Has there ever been a time when I've been going through a rehearsal and panicked? I'm not sure that I ever got Malvolio. Sam very sweetly says 'Oh no, you did.' Sam's very good at calming me down and saying 'It's going to be fine, don't worry,' but I do remember being quite panicked about that because we were also pressed for time on that one."

As much as he appreciates the ensemble working process ("It sounds utopian: but nothing is right and nothing is wrong") his experience on the play itself sounds less than appealing, precisely because of the role he was playing. "I found *Twelfth Night* a very cold play actually. It's like the old joke about what *Romeo and Juliet* is about: 'Oh, it's about this Nurse who...' says the actor playing the Nurse. I admit that it's absolutely from Malvolio's perspective though I do find it a very vicious play. *Uncle Vanya*, although it's very desperate at the end, is beating, absolutely beating with passion. From my perspective *Twelfth Night* just wasn't. Although I loved doing *Twelfth Night* and the process of rehearsals, it was a very remote experience. If you play Malvolio you're very, very isolated."

In any event, Malvolio exits in Act III, Scene 4 in yellow stockings, still fervently believing that his status is elevated and that the secret conduct between him and Olivia will soon be revealed to the other servants. "You are idle, shallow things; I am not of your element. You shall know more hereafter." With Olivia unaware of the letter trick and now under the belief that Malvolio's peculiar behaviour is the result of his being possessed, Sir Toby, Fabian and Maria resolve to have him bound and incarcerated in a dark house.

In the dark house scene (Act IV, Scene 2), Malvolio vehemently denies that he is mad, as everyone supposes. In Sam's production, Simon portrayed him in a state of actually questioning whether or not he had gone mad. "It wasn't deliberate in finding a softer side of him, but I wanted it to be a genuine worry. The scene that Shakespeare leaves out is the scene where Malvolio is caught. Is it left out because to see Malvolio react, presumably angrily, to the fact that he's been tricked is limiting to the possible responses that Malvolio might have later, which is that he's not sure, he's just not sure if he may have gone mad?"

Throughout the scene, Malvolio is taunted by Feste the clown, with whom he has had an altercation in his first appearance in Act I, Scene 5. Feste appears at the dark house, firstly in the guise of Sir Topas the curate and then as himself, in order to amuse Sir Toby, Maria and himself before eventually helping Malvolio to the ink, light and paper to write the letter that Olivia will receive in the final scene of the play. The punishment of being bound and kept in a dark house and taunted by the fool is, as Simon describes "a comic version of the awful tortures you read about in totalitarian states: sleep deprivation, light deprivation, continuous noise or whatever. That's sort of what he's suffering. I think it's desperately cruel; it's way beyond what he should be suffering."

Simon also believes that the scene of Malvolio's capture, prior to his imprisonment in the dark house, is also left out because "a normal sane man's reaction – shame and anger and aggression – would limit the possibility in the last scene too. That awful last moment when he's appealing to Olivia: this *is* your handwriting. You can't accuse me of being mad." With his own letter apparently suggesting that his sanity is intact, Malvolio is brought before Olivia in the presence of the Duke Orsino to challenge her about the letter he still supposes she penned. "It's sort of agent provocateur on the part of Toby and Maria. Anyone can fall for that. It's like Parolles in *All's Well That Ends Well*: 'Who cannot be crush'd with a plot.' It's so unfair, so unfair."

This sense of unfairness manifested itself in Malvolio's chilling final exit, which confirmed the character's place at the dark centre of the comedy. Sam distinctly remembers Simon's deliberate subversion of the audience's expectation as he left the stage. "It was not comically undignified. It was like someone scraping their fingernails across the blackboard in the middle of a violin concerto. It silenced the audience. You could hear a pin drop. It wasn't funny and it wasn't sentimental. It was a statement of intent."

MALVOLIO I'll be revenged on the whole pack of you.

(V.i.375)

"And you felt that he would be revenged. You didn't think that it was hollow. Simon is very skilled at introducing darkness into the light and light into the darkness."

THE WINTER'S TALE

"If you really feel the verse then it does have a beauty and energy all of its own"

THE WINTER'S TALE by WILLIAM SHAKESPEARE
FIRST PERFORMANCE: Harvey Theater, Brooklyn Academy of Music, New York, January 2009
SUBSEQUENT PERFORMANCES:
Singapore Repertory Theatre, 26-31 March 2009
The Edge, Auckland, 4-12 April 2009
Teatro Español, Madrid, 18-29 April 2009
Ruhrfestspiele Recklinghausen, Germany, 3-13 May 2009
The Athens & Epidaurus Festival, Greece, 21-22 Aug 2009

CAST

SIMON RUSSELL BEALE	Leontes
MICHAEL BRAUN	Dion/Florizel
MORVEN CHRISTIE	Mamillius/Perdita
SINEAD CUSACK	Paulina
RICHARD EASTON	Old Shepherd/Time
REBECCA HALL	Hermione
JOSH HAMILTON	Polixenes
ETHAN HAWKE	Autolycus
PAUL JESSON	Camillo
AARON KROHN	Servant
DAKIN MATTHEWS	Antigonus/Shepherd
MARK NELSON	Lord/Mariner/Shepherd
CHARLOTTE PARRY	Lady in Waiting/Mopsa
JESSICA POLLERT-SMITH	Dorcas
GARY POWELL	Cleomenes/Jailer /Bear/Shepherd
TOBIAS SEGAL	Young Shepherd
HANNAH STOKELY	Emilia/Shepherdess

CREATIVE TEAM

SAM MENDES	Director
ANTHONY WARD	Set Designer
CATHERINE ZUBER	Costume Designer
PAUL PYANT	Lighting
PAUL ARDITTI	Sound
MARK BENNETT	Music
DAN LIPTON	Music Director
JOSH PRINCE	Choreographer

"Sam Mendes' longest suit as a theatre director is micromanagement. As an actor in a student show he directed more than 20 years ago I watched, fascinated, as he showed his company semiotic, intellectual and emotional paths through the knottiest play text, getting us to understand it and to convey that understanding to an audience. Now, as a spectator, I relish the same skills in him. And in Simon Russell Beale he has an actor whose intuition and abilities match his own. Beale can strike two or three different moods in the same line and sometimes in the same instant, showing us the complexities and contradictions of a character. As the delusionally jealous Leontes in The Winter's Tale, *he observes his own disgusted insecurity almost as closely as he does the imagined intimacies between his wife Hermione and best friend Polixenes. When he realises how unwarranted his fervour was, but only after the abandonment of his newborn daughter and the death of his son and supposedly also of his wife, his repentance and mortification are in the selfsame key as his jealousy had been."*

(Ian Shuttleworth, *The Financial Times*, 11 June 2009)

Shakespeare's late plays *Pericles, The Winter's Tale, Cymbeline* and *The Tempest*, sometimes grouped as 'the romances', are triumphs of combining historical forms and old-fashioned source material with experimental dramaturgy. They all oscillate between the comedic and tragic and each one deals in one way or another with the pain of loss or separation and concludes with reconciliation and redemption. Each play has its own unique and vastly different qualities, not least of all in landscape but also in time: whereas the action of *The Tempest* operates within the Aristotelian 'Unities' of a single location within a single day, *The Winter's Tale* takes us from the kingdoms of Sicilia to Bohemia and back again across a time frame of sixteen years, with the gap uneasily bridged by a monologue from Time, acting as chorus, at the top of Act IV.

The late plays also show Shakespeare experimenting not only with form but also with the rhythms and language in a way that makes Antony Sher compare him to "a master jazz musician" and this is particularly true of *The Winter's Tale*. This isn't one of Shakespeare's early plays or a piece by Marlowe which is concretely locked into the structure of the ten beats in an iambic pentameter line.

The central character, Leontes, king of Sicilia, believes his pregnant wife Hermione and his old friend Polixenes, the king of Bohemia, are lovers and that the child she is carrying is not actually his. The physiological responses he experiences in his jealous state are represented within the rhythms and tempi of the text. "It's like he's retching up language, it's that contorted. He's physically incapacitated, and his heart is beating too fast. He's having palpitations. He says 'I have tremor cordis on me; my heart dances, but not for joy, not joy'. It's all there in the language," suggests Sam. If you're not willing to play within the structure of these experimental rhythms, Simon argues, and you stick to the rigidity of an iambic pentameter line, "things like Leontes could be really, really incomprehensible."

Usually Sam is very strict about the speaking of verse from a technical perspective, particularly at the beginning of rehearsals. "We don't do lessons in what an iambic pentameter line is, but if you abuse the verse too much he'll be on to you. We didn't talk so much in those terms with *The Winter's Tale* because Rebecca Hall's verse speaking as you'd expect is impeccable, Sinead Cusack has straight down the line classical delivery, Paul Jesson is one of the best verse speakers in the country and half the play is in prose anyway!"

As the transatlantic company of The Bridge Project started to cohere, there was a slight hesitation from the American actors, who are traditionally in awe of English Shakespearean actors, particularly in relation to Simon. As Sam remembers "Simon takes these great long passages of Leontes' and he somehow unlocks them in a way that is so deceptively easy. The Americans in the company had a sense that 'Oh, well, Simon is just born doing this. The English actors just know how to do this.' And I wanted to say 'No, no, no, it's just Simon's skill. It isn't that easy!'"

This production opened in Mamillius' nursery rather than in Leontes' bedroom as he struggled with insomnia as was originally intended. This was a similar environment to *The Cherry Orchard* with which it was twinned in The Bridge Project; the two plays linked through the significant theme of lost children. Leontes' young son Mamillus 'introduces' the tale with lines borrowed from Act II:

> "Pray you sit by us
> And tell's a tale. / Merry or sad shall't be?
> As merry as you will.
> A sad tale's best for winter."
>
> (II.i.21-24)

Into this nursery enter Leontes, Hermione and their guest Polixenes, as if they have just been sat to dinner and they are retiring for discussion prior to going to bed, brandies in hands, as Leontes observes every move that Hermione and Polixenes make together. It is not clear from the text whether the evidence that he accumulates and later expresses about their supposed affair – whispering, leaning cheek to cheek, meeting noses, horsing foot on foot, skulking in corners, and the provocative "kissing with inside lip" – are internal stage directions i.e. the audience should see Hermione and Polixenes engaging in these activities, or whether they are inventions of Leontes own hyperactive and potentially diseased imagination.

One approach that Sam considered was the possibility of showing both versions of the scene one after the other, first as the events actually occurred in 'reality' and then how Leontes views and distorts them. In this sense, the play would have a deliberate false-start, as it is the effects of Leontes' jealousy and the actions that Leontes takes because of it that drive the plot forward. Simon's rather withering response to the suggestion was "So... we have to do it twice?" The idea wasn't carried forward.

In the actual production, the lighting state changed to a deep blue and Leontes stepped down onto the apron of the stage, removing himself from the bounds of the nursery set to deliver "Too hot, too hot! To mingle friendship far is mingling bloods..." In the same way that the blue light bathed the stage in *The Tempest* on Ariel's first entrance to suggest another plane of existence and an uninterruptable collusion between Prospero and his servant, so here we are taken into Leontes mind and he speaks directly to us through soliloquy and we see the version of events skewed from his perspective.

For Simon, the idea of Leontes' jealousy was only ever a starting point and automatically led on to other 'micro-arguments.' Is Leontes jealous before the play starts or does it arrive suddenly and without warning just prior to the first soliloquy? The answers to this question obviously lead on to other questions and each of the various avenues needed to be explored throughout rehearsal.

Finally Leontes confides his suspicions to one of his lords, Camillo, and charges him with the task of murdering Polixenes. "Dost not think my wife is slippery?" he asks. "I take an enormous amount of time over that and it's just not right," admits Simon. "'Dost not think my wife is.... slippery?' It's just not right, it doesn't need it. Perhaps a half beat but not as much as I was giving. If you do that too much, you can feel the verse disappear through your fingers. You can feel the substructure of it and the support it gives you disappearing. If you really feel the verse then it does have a beauty and energy all of its own."

In a strange way, Sam and Simon have reached a stage in their relationship that's akin to this quality within the late plays. They have twenty years worth of shared experience across comedy and tragedy, Shakespeare and Chekhov, and a mutual understanding and respect for the process of collaboration. To an extent their working practices have synthesised so that they are communicating through their own type of jazz. "He is one of the few actors I would talk to whilst he's acting, quietly, during the rehearsals or a run through."

"I'll say something to him or I'll make a gesture," Sam begins to demonstrate, "and he'll know what I mean." He might turn his finger in a small circle to mean keep going or explore that root more. He will point upwards to mean you can pitch that higher. He'll hold his palm out to mean stop, you can hold that pause for longer than you're doing now. "I don't think about it. I just do it instinctively. That's evolved over a long, long period."

In rehearsals Sam likes to use methods of communication that are non-verbal. In *The Winter's Tale* he had control of the prop baby Perdita's crying through a little keyboard of sound effects next to him. It's an approach Sam has used as early as *Troilus and Cressida* where he would punctuate selected scenes with a drum. "It was an odd way of focussing the actors within the scene even if I wasn't intending to underscore it in the final production." To a lesser, and far cheekier, extent the repeated deployment of the fart machine through *Twelfth Night* could be seen as a way of generating the necessary playful atmosphere when rehearsing a comedy.

For the scene where Leontes is presented with his newborn daughter by Paulina (played by Sinead Cusack), Sam was controlling the baby's crying. He was certain that he wanted the baby to be a genuine presence on stage rather than just a bundle. During a run-through of the scene, Sam deliberately made the baby cry on two unusual occasions when Simon wasn't expecting it.

"Other actors might stop and say 'is that when you're going to make the baby cry in the scene?' Simon knows what I'm doing; he knows I'm trying to throw him off his centre to see what's interesting. His thought process is in milliseconds. He knows I'm trying to tell him that this is the moment that Leontes is thrown off his centre and has to contemplate it and think of it as a real child. He runs through the options: 'Maybe I should look at it, maybe I should hold it...'"

Sam might also try to throw Simon off his centre in character by asking Cusack to hand the baby to him and make him take it. Simon wouldn't only follow through with where this suggestion takes him, he would also acknowledge the idea behind the suggestion. "It's not just about the exploration, but he takes the idea and reads it backwards and forwards throughout a whole scene in the moment that it's suggested. Simon's speed of analysis – what it would mean for the journey of the whole character in the whole play – is exceptional."

As in their production of *Uncle Vanya* the action in the third act of *The Winter's Tale* took place across a long table that stretched across the width of the stage. We were not in a family scene of Russian estate here but in the formal and austere setting of court, as Leontes brings Hermione up on the charge of adultery. It is clear that Leontes wants to conduct a public hearing in an attempt to prove that he is not being tyrannical. In doing so, Simon was clear that he needed to resist playing the irrational side of Leontes' jealousy. The character believes that he is pursuing a rational course of action.

LEONTES This sessions, to our great grief we pronounce
Even pushes 'gainst our heart – the party tried,
The daughter of a king, our wife and one
Of us too much belov'd. Let us be clear'd
Of being tyrannous, since we so openly
Proceed in justice, which shall have due course,
Even to the guilt or the purgation.
Produce the prisoner.

(III.ii.1-8)

This passage brought up another interesting note about the speaking of the verse. "Normally I would run the line straight through: 'The daughter of a king, our wife and one of us too much beloved.' On this occasion I stuck with the meter. 'The daughter of a king, our wife and one // of us too much belov'd.' Leontes is wondering how to phrase this. It was a tiny residual beat but it was there in the performance."

"Don't get me wrong, I absolutely respect the intention of the verse. You have to acknowledge that it's there and that it is not prose, but I don't believe that it's an infallible rule that Shakespeare will always help you. I think that's a bit of a tease really. Sometimes he does, perhaps most of the times he does, but sometimes he doesn't, especially in the late plays. My job is to make it clear at first hearing if that's at all possible. *The Winter's Tale* is difficult enough as it is."

In the course of Hermione's trial, Leontes consults the oracle of the Gods for the truth of his accusations. The oracle pronounces Hermione chaste, Polixenes blameless, Camillo true and Leontes a jealous tyrant. To the disbelief of all assembled Leontes commits the gravest sacrilege by proclaiming that there is no truth in the oracle. In this production he raised his arms to heaven as if directly challenging the gods to disavow the truth of his accusations. Nothing happened and Leontes allowed himself to laugh at his own righteousness. It was only when Leontes thought that he'd got away with it that the servant arrived with the news of Mamillius' death.

Hermione swoons on stage and is escorted away and Leontes desperately apologises to the Gods for angering them. It is here that

Simon had to make the emotional jump with Leontes. "It's an obvious moment really but it's the point where Paulina returns to Leontes to announce the death of the queen and Leontes is actively at his lowest. 16 years later it's not so active, but here he wants to be dead so he's obviously very low."

PAULINA I say she's dead; I'll swear it. If word nor oath
Prevail not, go and see. If you can bring
Tincture or lustre in her lip, her eye
Heat outwardly or breath within, I'll serve you
As I would do the gods. But, O thou tyrant!
Do not repent these things, for they are heavier
Than all thy woes can stir; therefore betake thee
To nothing but despair. A thousand knees
Ten thousand years together, naked, fasting
Upon a barren mountain, and still winter
In storm perpetual, could not move the gods
To look that way thou wert.

LEONTES Go on, go on.

(III.ii.200-211)

Simon became particularly fascinated by Paulina's speech. "It's like a mallet; like a series of great sucker punches one after the other. 'A thousand knees / ten thousand years together / naked / fasting...' It's like Leontes is being hit in the stomach again and again and again. His next line 'Go on' came out as this sort of roar. I suppose I knew that Sam was waiting for something like that: an absolute loss of dignity. It was a howl of pain, which I was never able to rediscover again completely in performance. It just came up from the gut one rehearsal: shrieking at the moon really."

The staging placed Leontes downstage looking upstage towards Paulina, in a similar format to how Simon had hoped Leontes would be seen as the lonely man at his desk. Perhaps it is due to his reticence of big emotional outpourings, but it requires a certain bravery from an actor to turn their back on an audience during a pivotal onstage moment. For Simon it's a personal challenge that goes right the way back to his early career at the Royal Court. "I remember Bill Gaskill saying to me that the only person that could act with their back was Peggy Ashcroft and I thought 'Right...'"

It's a formation that is re-evoked in the staging for the final reconciliation scene. This time, the live Hermione, secluded by Paulina during the sixteen year passage of time until her daughter Perdita is recovered, is placed in the downstage centre hotspot with her back to the audience posing as a statue, in the same position where Leontes howled in pain for her passing.

Intellectually, this scene of reconciliation is a flip version to the scene of loss that is the conclusion to the trial in the same way that the Queen Elizabeth scene flips the Lady Anne scene in *Richard III*. One deals with the death and despair, the other with rebirth and hope. Sam's staging directly tied in to that intellectual construct, with the 'statue' that rebuilds the relationships occupying the space that the destructive Leontes repented. On both occasions Paulina acts as the intermediary.

The return to Sicilia from Bohemia began with an image of Leontes and Paulina sat like Derby and Joan on a bench. "I felt that it was wrong that this misery should somehow be fresh, as if he'd just come from whipping himself at a chapel or whatever. This was old and dead, these sixteen years of misery. That was what I was looking for through the image of Phillip II – and it is interesting that it's always an image – something that represented that."

For the reconciliation scene itself, Shakespeare tries to convince us that it can happen naturalistically and that an allegorical reading is difficult, but for Simon "the naturalistic details are a barrier. You need an open, receptive mind at this stage of the play; transcendental, suspended disbelief and absolute forgiveness. The last scene is almost literally a miracle happening. I use the word 'miracle' a lot when talking about *The Winter's Tale*."

THE CHERRY ORCHARD

"I picked the chair up and hurled it right across the rehearsal room"

THE CHERRY ORCHARD by ANTON CHEKHOV
In a new version of the play by TOM STOPPARD
FIRST PERFORMANCE: Harvey Theater, Brooklyn Academy of Music, New York, January 2009
SUBSEQUENT PERFORMANCES:
The Edge, Auckland, 4-12 April 2009
Teatro Español, Madrid, 18-29 April 2009
Ruhrfestspiele Recklinghausen, Germany, 3-13 May 2009

CAST

SIMON RUSSELL BEALE	Lopakhin
MICHAEL BRAUN	Ensemble
SELINA CADELL	Charlotta Ivanovna
MORVEN CHRISTIE	Anya
SINEAD CUSACK	Ranevskaya
RICHARD EASTON	Firs
REBECCA HALL	Varya
JOSH HAMILTON	Yasha
ETHAN HAWKE	Trofimov
PAUL JESSON	Gaev
AARON KROHN	Post Office Clerk
DAKIN MATTHEWS	Simeonov-Pishchik
MARK NELSON	Station Master
CHARLOTTE PARRY	Dunyasha
JESSICA POLLERT-SMITH	Ensemble
GARY POWELL	Passer-by
TOBIAS SEGAL	Yepikhodov
HANNAH STOKELY	Ensemble

CREATIVE TEAM

SAM MENDES	Director
ANTHONY WARD	Set Designer
CATHERINE ZUBER	Costume Designer
PAUL PYANT	Lighting
PAUL ARDITTI	Sound
MARK BENNETT	Music
DAN LIPTON	Music Director
JOSH PRINCE	Choreographer

"Back in 2002 Sam Mendes departed the Donmar Warehouse after 10 brilliant years as artistic director with a double bill of Shakespeare's Twelfth Night *and Chekhov's* Uncle Vanya. *Now after too long an absence from the British stage, he returns with a new company, The Bridge Project, and another pairing of Shakespeare and Chekhov. Once again Simon Russell Beale, for my money this country's greatest stage actor, stars in both shows. [T]here is little hope in Chekhov's play, unless you are a rabid Marxist, which sees a family we have greatly come to care about heading for the most desperate of futures. Both dramas also concern the unbearable pain of lost children, and the deeply moving way Mendes depicts the pleasure and sorrow of family life marks a new maturity in his work as well as being a touching testament to his love for his own wife and children. The shows will be best remembered for Simon Russell Beale's wonderful performances. [...]* The Cherry Orchard, *translated with cheeky panache by Tom Stoppard ("Get thee to a scullery and may all my sinks be remembered" Lopakhin tells the housekeeper Varya). Yet somehow Russell Beale endows even this vulgar, workaholic businessman with the soul of a poet."*

(Charles Spencer, *The Telegraph*, 10 June 2009)

Sam had intended for his second staging of *The Tempest* in 2008 to be one half of the inaugural season for The Bridge Project, a new transatlantic company encompassing the best talent from the United Kingdom, Ireland and the United States. When the lead actor Stephen Dillane had to withdraw for personal reasons, the project was postponed by a year and opened at the Brooklyn Academy of Music, New York in 2009 with *The Cherry Orchard*, also his second production of that play.

When casting *The Cherry Orchard*, a similar situation to the offer of a part in *The Tempest* arose, only in reverse. Whenever he is working on two plays in repertory, Sam cleverly balances the two plays so that they complement and contrast each other. The working process can subtly reveal similarities and common threads that offer reflections both for the audience and for the actors. Here, *The Cherry Orchard* was twinned with *The Winter's Tale*. Both are late plays by their respective authors, and among their many themes, is the loss of innocence and the death of a child. It is also imperative the line of parts the actors are offered are also complementary. Sam is equally adept at creating a package of two parts that will be both attractive to an actor and will work for the production. It's often a very pragmatic as well as an artistic decision.

In this case, Leontes, the King of Sicilia in *The Winter's Tale*, was twinned with Lopakhin, the lower class peasant who has grafted his way to success in *The Cherry Orchard*. This double had already been worked out when Sam offered the line of parts to Simon. Simon was excited and accepted, though there was a level of anxiety about being asked to play Lopakhin. Sam thought that Simon looked like a Lopakhin and had the right aggression for the part; Simon agreed that he looked like a Lopakhin but he didn't sound like one. He was much more suited to portraying the intelligent, linguistically rich, royal Leontes than the dullard businessman.

Aware of Simon's anxiety, and perhaps even scared that he'd miscast Simon himself, Sam had another casting rethink and made another brief phone call to check that Simon was sure about accepting the role. He even had an alternative casting suggestion, and this time he offered Gaev, the brother of Ranevskaya who owns the estate that the cherry orchard is part of, who has a tendency to punctuate many of his thoughts – as well as dramatic moments in the play – with a running commentary on an imaginary game of billiards. It was the role that Simon originally thought that Sam would offer him, and would certainly have been a more comfortable fit for the actor.

The facility to explore these alternative casting possibilities comes from considerable forward planning. Since 1998, Sam has had a film and theatre schedule to balance; Simon is usually committed to productions with long runs planned. In the case of *The Cherry Orchard* there was a two year period between the initial offer of Lopakhin and the first day of rehearsals.

Although Simon had genuinely been worried about how he would go about playing Lopakhin, he had already begun reading through the part and his brain was alive with the numerous possibilities, ready to begin work in the rehearsal room. He wanted to seize the chance to approach something that made him worried, something that was out of his comfort zone. Sam concurred and they decided to commit to the slightly riskier option.

However, Simon's anxiety about 'not sounding like a Lopakhin' remained. Lopakhin was indeed out of his comfort zone, and like the characters of Man in Pinter's *Landscape* and Undershaft in Shaw's *Major Barbara* which he'd both recently played at the NT, Lopakhin fed into Simon's self criticism of not being able to do accents and not being able to play alpha males. To combat this, Simon worked through many rehearsals giving Lopakhin a rough London accent. It leant a suggestion of Lopakhin as the self-made man, clawing his way up the rich list through a ruthless combination of grit and determination: Chekhov's answer to Alan Sugar, perhaps. Sam was absolutely insistent that the accent was unnecessary and eventually squashed it. What remained in Simon's performance was only a vague trace of an accent. He slightly altered his voice to give it a rougher edge.

The rehearsal process for *The Cherry Orchard* differed from that of the 1993 *Tempest* in many ways. This was a single ensemble performing two plays in repertory: *The Cherry Orchard* was twinned with *The Winter's Tale*. For the first (and to date only) time, Sam and Simon were working with the writer in the rehearsal room. Tom Stoppard had adapted Chekhov's text and was present at rehearsals. This can significantly change the dynamic of the rehearsal environment, and a tendency develops of asking the writer to provide the answers, sometimes on a line by line basis. This can be particularly true when the writer is as intelligent as Stoppard, but even he occasionally found himself scrambling for the literal translation for assistance.

The Cherry Orchard was also a continuation of Sam's evolving rehearsal process. Moving away from a more traditional system that he used at the RSC of calling the actors for each scene as they are required in the schedule, and using solus calls to work with individual actors independently of the rest of the company, Sam has nurtured a more inclusive, ensemble approach to working. All of the actors are called all of the time and are all able to contribute equally throughout the duration of the rehearsal process, regardless of whether their character features in a scene or not. He also uses a complex structure of games to cohere, relax – and on occasion, embarrass – the members of the ensemble.

On the first day of *The Cherry Orchard* rehearsals Simon was the first person to be asked to stand up to play a game in front of the ensemble, along with Charlotte Parry who appears opposite Simon at the very opening of the play in the role of the housemaid Dunyasha. Mercifully, the game is not too embarrassing for them: Sam asks them to play the scene with Charlotte as Lopakhin and Simon as Dunyasha.

Lopakhin, the 'little peasant' who has grown up into a self-made man with plenty of capital, opens the play having fallen asleep and missed the opportunity to welcome Ranevskaya from the train. She is the owner of a great estate which includes the titular cherry orchard, and who showed Lopakhin some kindness in their youth despite their class difference. Now he is a person of great wealth and she is experiencing serious financial difficulties. Lopakhin believes the solution is to give the land over to a series of development plots for summer cottages to bring in money against her debts.

"It's a nuisance, I was looking forward to seeing you and having a talk – you still look as wonderful as ever," says Lopakhin about his own imminently departing train. Attempting to bring out the subtext of Lopakhin's suggested love for Ranevskaya as much as possible, Simon locks in to the idea of 'having a talk' and makes it a euphemism, but during one preview performance in New York, he pushes this a little too far and it is clearly not to Sam's liking. "It sounds absolutely salacious" is the note, which is accompanied by some merciless teasing and 'having a talk' becomes another of the pair's many running jokes.

At the next performance, sulking a little and burned by the teasing, Simon dutifully takes the note and avoids the euphemism. But he now feels that the moment is somehow empty. The following night, he is determined to reach for his original thought on that line, but

Sam's mocking voice rings heavily in his ears and Simon simply can't go through with it. "I've never been able to do it the same again after that," he says cheekily, apparently not through want of trying. "I had a perfectly good reason for doing the line that way but Sam obviously thought it wasn't right. It's gone. Oh, well, it's not a huge loss."

Lopakhin is still attempting to 'have a talk' with Ranevskaya when we see him again in Act Two, desperately trying to convince her and her brother Gaev that action is required and that the estate must be divided up into separate plots of profitable land. It's in this exchange that we first hear of Deriganov, a character we never see on stage and who is mentioned only three times in the entire play; all we learn about him is that he is a millionaire who wants to buy the estate and will be attending the auction in person.

Yet even this small detail can be used to great effect during a lengthy tour or rehearsal process, when actors can lock into a particular pattern and rhythm and performances can begin to feel heavy, flat and tired. To prevent this, as we have seen, Sam cunningly poses questions that are designed to give actors something specific to think about that they may not have considered before. For *The Cherry Orchard*, this was framed as "Things I want to believe." His proposition to Simon was "I want to believe that Lopakhin loathes Deriganov." Though it's probable that even when put into action this small suggestion will not register with an audience and may seem insignificant in the broader arc of the play, exercises like this offer great benefits to the actors and aid the overall performance. It makes an actor engage their brain and helps to keep a performance fresh and alive, placing a minute twist or spin on these two or three lines.

It's during this scene that it becomes obvious that Lopakhin's repressed love for Ranevskaya will never be requited, yet her adopted daughter Varya is desperately in love with him. Lopakhin seems less enthusiastic at the prospect of Varya being his wife.

RANEVSKAYA What you need to do, my dear, is get married.

LOPAKHIN Yes... true enough.

RANEVSKAYA To someone like our Varya. She's a good girl.

LOPAKHIN She is.

RANEVSKAYA She comes from simple folk, so she can work all day long, but the main thing is she's in love with you. And you've liked her for a long time, haven't you?

LOPAKHIN Well, yes, I'm not against it. She's a good girl.

(*The Cherry Orchard*, Act II)

In Act III, we learn the fate of the cherry orchard, with Lopakhin returning from the auction where the threatened estate was up for sale having purchased it. He then has a long speech recounting the events of the auction and ruminating on how far his lineage has come now that he is the owner of the estate where his family were kept as slaves. During early performances, Simon was worried that he was taking too much time over this moment and tried to hurry it along, aware that there were twenty people on stage waiting for him to finish and an audience of one thousand listening to him every night.

During particularly dramatic moments such as this, actors can have a tendency to indulge too much in a certain feeling, in an attempt to ensure that both audience and fellow actors grasp the significance of the event being discussed. It is usually the responsibility of the director to ensure that the actor has the requisite momentum to drive through the argument of the speech without wallowing in unnecessary emotions to the detriment of the dramatic effect. This is no different in Sam and Simon's relationship, but on this occasion, Sam had spotted that Simon was rushing and encouraged him to slow down, particularly during the line "The cherry orchard is mine! It's mine! My God, ladies and gentlemen, the cherry orchard is mine!" In the arc of the play this is a vital turning point. "You're not prepared for each thought as you go through it and you're not fully investing. Really slow down and wait for the thought to strike."

At the end of the speech, Lopakhin is led towards the ballroom demanding dancing and music, but bumps into a table on his exit, nearly knocking over a candelabrum. In the physical production, Simon topples a chair and proceeds around the perimeter of the stage violently knocking over the remaining chairs positioned there in quick succession before proudly stating, "Don't worry, I can pay for everything." The toppling of the chairs is another of the unscripted theatrical gestures which can illuminate everything that has been hitherto unspoken within the scene or throughout the play. Sam arrived at the idea very early in the rehearsal process following a particularly aggressive version of the speech Simon gave.

One of the disadvantages of having the full ensemble in the rehearsal room all of the time is that a level of frustration can develop amongst the actors when the focus is on scenes in which they are not involved. When an actor is grappling with a large or complex part, a sense of anxiety can develop when you're not working directly on the role, even if the work is an opportunity for reflection during time out of the rehearsal space. However, this mixture of anxiety and resentment can have unexpected consequences. Simon arrived at the rehearsal room in a bad mood, certain that he wasn't going to have anything to do for the entire day, but due to a quirk in the schedule, the company reached the scene of the play that includes Lopakhin's long speech.

"I was really pissed off that day," Simon recalls. "It just so happens that we'd got to that scene and I'd learnt it as I've started learning parts much earlier now because I'm older and it's not as easy as it used to be and I hate being on the floor with a book. At the end of the speech, I tripped over the chair. I picked the chair up and hurled it right across the rehearsal room. It was very childish, because it was my own grumpiness on display and not Lopakhin's. That huge aggression..." Yet, Sam seized on the event and developed it into a startling theatrical moment.

Following that aggression is the more elegiac Act IV. It's a point of departure; it's both the end of the play and the last time that the characters will see each other for a long time. It is winter; a time when the estate is closed due to the seasonal lifestyle of this community. As everyone says their goodbyes, there is a final encounter between Varya and Lopakhin. They discuss their plans for the future; Varya has accepted a position as a housekeeper for the Ragulin family forty miles away, while the workaholic Lopakhin is once again heading to Kharkov on the next train.

At this point in the production Lopakhin bends down on one knee next to her, looking deep into Varya's expectant eyes. It's another unscripted moment, and is a suggestion that the long-anticipated marriage proposal is about to be made. "This time last year the snow had come, do you remember? But this year it's sunny and calm. Cold, though. Three degrees of frost," Lopakhin says, with unexpected poetry. "I didn't look" responds Varya and there is a long pause. She feels she needs to fill the silence. "And, anyway, our thermometer is broken." As the mundane details of everyday life and Varya's workaday mentality invade the longed-for moment, Lopakhin is called from offstage and hurries away as though he has long been waiting for an excuse to escape. It is a moment both funny and uncomfortable filled with a brief tenderness but without the promise of a happy ending.

Each character exits towards their life independent of one another, Lopakhin announcing that everything is finished for the house "until the spring," when the characters will return from their respective ways of life to congregate again, in much the same way Sam and Simon's 'neat' relationship sees them separated until they arrive for the next production to collaborate again.

"So – goodbye. Time to go. We may turn up our noses at each other, but life goes on regardless. The only time my mind is at peace is when I work without stopping for hours on end. Then I feel I know why I'm here."

(Lopakhin, *The Cherry Orchard*, Act IV)

NEAR MISSES AND FUTURE PRODUCTIONS

"I haven't had a single thought about it yet, except for shitting myself"

At a recent platform, the Director of the National Theatre Sir Nicholas Hytner was asked in a question and answer session if actors ever ask to do specific plays. "No. Except once: Simon Russell Beale did say he wanted to do *King Lear*." Simon swiftly counters that. "It wasn't my idea! I was deputed to mention it to Nick. I rush to say that because it was Sam's idea. I was at the National and he was heading back to America, so I mentioned it to Nick and Sam followed it up."

With the large Shakespearean and comparable roles, selecting your leading actor is almost always the first part of the process in generating a production. As an extension of the casting process, Simon is always passive in this, waiting for the suggestion to come from Sam. "If I had a passionate idea to do a part I would say so. There was a time when I thought I'd like to do Doctor Faustus when I was a younger man and I said to Sam that I'd like to do it, but that was a five minute conversation. Firstly, what the hell do you do with that play? It's such a difficult one to do. That's probably the only time I've said anything directly to him."

Sometimes, the desire to be involved in projects extends beyond identifying those roles that they can work on together. When Sam was considering television productions of some of Shakespeare's plays, Simon recommended himself as dramaturg, having already completed a suitable edit for *The Tempest* and taking charge of which texts would be the most appropriate to use. Sam believes that this was not with a view to finding himself cast in the television productions, but because of his joy in being a part of the Shakespeare continuum.

"Most actors are not academically minded. Simon has that analytical capacity which runs in tandem with his own emotional need to perform and to be admired, which every actor has whether they say they do or they don't. He's very honest about it: he wants to be part of the debate. He wants people to be talking about his Hamlet or his Iago or his Richard III, because he's rightly proud of them and he feels that he wants to make his mark on that landscape of Shakespearean roles that he admires so much."

"He's worked unbelievably hard for 30 years. He's working his way through the Shakespearean canon, the Chekhovian canon and many other plays, with a deepening understanding and a growing craft that is almost unparalleled now for someone of his generation. It is a combination of emotional and intellectual hunger for those plays: to play everything and to understand everything."

It has recently been announced that the Shakespeare television project will come to fruition, with Sam commissioned by the BBC to create screen versions of *Richard II*, *Henry IV Parts 1 and 2*, and *Henry V*. Richard Eyre and Rupert Goold have been announced to direct alongside Sam, who will be Executive Producer. And Simon has indeed been named as Associate Producer.

Given their respective busy schedules, Sam and Simon begin planning their next productions far in advance. In theatre terms, Simon is nearly always involved in relatively long runs on each project he undertakes, and Sam has to balance his film and theatre careers. Sam first approached Simon about *The Winter's Tale* and *The Cherry Orchard* two years in advance when Simon was doing *Spamalot* in London. Sam already knew that the first phase of The Bridge Project was going to be *Hamlet* and *The Tempest* with Stephen Dillane and he offered Simon parts in the next phase. "I can't remember why Sam didn't want me to be in the first one. I may have been unavailable – I'm hoping that was the reason! I did say jokingly 'I hope you miss me.'" *Hamlet* and *The Tempest* were subsequently delayed. "I didn't curse it!" The second phase of The Bridge Project with Stephen Dillane was eventually *As You Like It* and *The Tempest*.

For Sam's farewell double bill of *Uncle Vanya* and *Twelfth Night* at the Donmar, Simon was also approached fairly far in advance. "I'd never worked at the Donmar and it was a great regret of mine and I think Sam rather sweetly wanted me to be involved in the final ones." If circumstances had been different, Simon may well have been involved in Sam's first production at the Donmar.

ASSASSINS Music and Lyrics by STEPHEN SONDHEIM
Book by JAMES LAPINE
FIRST PERFORMANCE: Donmar Warehouse, London, 22 October 1992

CAST		**CREATIVE TEAM**	
SIMON RUSSELL BEALE	Samuel Byck	SAM MENDES	Director

"Yes! I tried to get him to do *Assassins*," beams Sam enthusiastically. "I tried to get him to play Sam Byck but it was impossible at the time because he was doing *Richard III*. I mentioned it around the same time but it wasn't an offer and a retraction. It simply became clear that *Richard III* would be on tour because it came into the Donmar shortly afterwards."

At this point in time, the two collaborators had worked exclusively on Shakespeare. According to Simon the idea of doing a musical together did come from left field but, "I was so excited about Sam taking over the Donmar and I desperately wanted to be in his inaugural production; that mattered more than what the project actually was. Had I had the opportunity to think more about it I probably would have thought it was ridiculous. Though, I suppose he had heard me sing by that point."

"I would have loved to have done *Assassins*, although I literally couldn't have afforded it at that stage. I could afford it more now because of things like *Spamalot* but it would have been impossible then. Sam was very good about that: he understood I think. I simply couldn't do it. Once or twice he suggested something at the Donmar – it wasn't like he was hankering after me!"

In the eventual production, the role of Samuel Byck was brilliantly portrayed by Ciaran Hinds. According to Matt Wolf in his chronicle of Sam's tenure at the Donmar *Stepping into Freedom*, "played by Hinds, Byck seemed a crazed variant on Travis Bickle from *Taxi Driver*." Sam and Simon had first worked with Hinds when he played Achilles in *Troilus and Cressida* at the RSC. Ironically, Hinds had to return to the Donmar a week after the run of *Assassins* finished to take over the role of Richard III from Simon when he was incapacitated by a back injury.

OLIVER! Book, Music and Lyrics by LIONEL BART
FIRST PERFORMANCE: Theatre Royal Drury Lane, London

CAST		**CREATIVE TEAM**	
SIMON RUSSELL BEALE	Fagin	SAM MENDES	Director

It wasn't scheduling conflicts that prevented Sam from casting Simon as Fagin in his revival of *Oliver!* It was a decision by the producer. "At that stage Cameron Mackintosh felt that he needed a bigger name to open the show and it ended up being Jonathan Pryce."

"That was a pity," says Simon mournfully. "Fagin was such an odd idea. Only because I sat there imagining what Fagin would look like. Again I come back to the idea that if Sam thought I could do it then I could do it. At that stage in my career I was thinking 'I can't spend that long doing the same job,' when of course most people would give their left leg, as I would now, for a year-long project."

To this day they have not as yet collaborated together on a musical and there are currently no plans for them to do so. Independently both have worked successfully in musicals in the West End and on Broadway; since *Oliver!* Sam directed hugely successful revivals of *Cabaret* with Alan Cumming and *Gypsy* with Bernadette Peters and Simon starred as Voltaire and Pangloss in *Candide* and as King Arthur in *Spamalot*.

HAMLET by WILLIAM SHAKESPEARE
FIRST PERFORMANCE: Lyttelton Theatre, National Theatre, 15 July 2000

CAST		**CREATIVE TEAM**	
SIMON RUSSELL BEALE	Hamlet	SAM MENDES	Director

There is a long standing theatrical tradition of regarding the roles of Oswald in Ibsen's *Ghosts* and Konstantin in Chekhov's *The Seagull* as practice attempts leading up to tackling Hamlet in performance. Simon had already played Konstantin in Terry Hands' production – in which he famously took a full two minutes of silence to tear up his manuscripts before exiting the stage to shoot himself – when Sam first mentioned the idea of them working on a production of *Hamlet* together, during the tour of *Richard III*. Simon's next role was Oswald in Katie Mitchell's production of *Ghosts* for the RSC.

Having tackled the two 'preparatory' doomed youths, theatre journalists were already speculating on the possibility of Simon Russell Beale playing the Dane in a Sam Mendes production. "There was a newspaper article that said *Beale Heads for Elsinore*. It said Russell Beale is going to be doing *Hamlet* and because of my physicality and the fact that I'm not a heroic lead it was regarded as an odd idea and hopefully some people thought it was an interesting idea."

The first opportunity for the production to happen came in 1995 at the Donmar Warehouse. "We were very close to making it happen at the Donmar. Simon had agreed to do *Duchess of Malfi* in the West End when we would have been rehearsing. He always overworks. I wouldn't say too much, because he always proves he's capable of doing it, but I said 'You can't rehearse *Hamlet* in the day and do something else in the evenings. You're going to kill yourself.' You can't do it."

It seems that there are always two or more high profile productions of *Hamlet* occurring at the same time. Toby Stephens was playing Hamlet at the RSC in Michael Boyd's production around the same time that Ben Whishaw appeared at the Old Vic for Trevor Nunn. Most recently, Greg Doran's RSC production with David Tennant and Michael Grandage's near simultaneous Donmar in the West End production with Jude Law caused Nicholas Hytner to move back his planned National Theatre production with Rory Kinnear. Sam and Simon were left facing the same problem as they waited for the most opportune moment as their proposed production quickly garnered a reputation for being the most anticipated *Hamlet* not to be produced.

Six years after they had first discussed the possibility, tentative plans for a Donmar Warehouse production were revived. Then Sam's debut film was released. "When *American Beauty* happened for him I got an email saying that he'd have to drop out but that I should definitely do it. I absolutely understood, though I was disappointed obviously, but it was a new world for him. I don't suppose he ever thought that *American Beauty* would do what it did. The pressures on him were becoming intense and you can't do *Hamlet* under that set of circumstances."

With Sam's blessing, Simon approached Trevor Nunn, then Artistic Director for NT. "He said I don't think I'm the right person to direct you but I'm perfectly willing to put it on, which was very sweet of him though I think he had his doubts but good chap he decided to go with it." John Caird had directed Simon in *Money* by Edward Bulwer-Lytton and had always regarded Simon's performance as Alfred Evelyn as a sketch for their production of *Hamlet*. At the age of 39, Simon finally portrayed Hamlet in the 2000 National Theatre Production under Caird's direction. Sam is yet to direct a production of *Hamlet*.

"I think Sam himself would say that *Hamlet* isn't necessarily one of the ones that he felt he had to do. It's like *Macbeth*. I don't think he has any particular interest in *Macbeth*, which is where we differ a lot because I have quite a lot interest in both of those plays. He's also quite brave at that: about saying I don't think that this is right for me in my soul. It must be a difficult thing to judge because in any project you must be thinking 'I'm not sure about this.' When do you judge when the project is just not right? He was very worried about coming to see *Hamlet*. He came to my dressing room after the performance. There were no notes! He was very moved by it. It was weird because I don't think at that stage I'd done many Shakespeares without him."

Far from having "no notes" Sam regards this production as a major turning point for Simon. "His big breakthrough as an actor, in my opinion, was that production I did not direct though I wish I had. I think that Iago prepared him for it weirdly because it took him into a world of psychological realism that he had – up until then – not occupied in his classical work. There was a bit of mischief about his work up until that point, even with Ariel. Iago was just grown up. Shakespeare helps hugely because it's so psychologically acute and so well put together and so detailed."

"He'd gone into this tunnel of much more focused character psychology and then his mum died. He was very, very close to his mum who was a wonderful, lovely woman and I think that it absolutely took a piece of him away. And the grief of that manifested itself very much in *Hamlet*. I think that it changed him as a person and it changed him as an actor. I thought it was real, I didn't think it was fake. Although, I say that, his Konstantin was amazing as well. He's played the three Hamlet roles: Oswald in *Ghosts*, Konstanstin in *The Seagull* and Hamlet. Those three were all wonderful performances but Hamlet definitely changed him. The person I inherited after that was capable of playing Vanya, was capable of playing Leontes and is capable of Lear, Prospero, Falstaff, though I think that he could have played Falstaff, certainly in spirit, as a younger man."

Clearly the experiences portraying Oswald, Konstantin and Hamlet have had a positive impact on the work that Simon does with Sam, demonstrating that experiences outside the collaboration can positively inform and enrich future work.

For the future work, much furore has already been generated about the announcement of their latest project. The actor Sam West has often said that for most classical actors there is a 'Hamlet age' and a 'Lear age.' Though many people may agree that this is true, they probably wouldn't anticipate these ages being less than a decade apart in one career:

KING LEAR by WILLIAM SHAKESPEARE
FIRST PERFORMANCE: Olivier Theatre, National Theatre, London, 2013

CAST		**CREATIVE TEAM**	
SIMON RUSSELL BEALE	King Lear	SAM MENDES	Director

In the final act of David Hare's new version of *The Life of Galileo* by Bertolt Brecht, the director, Howard Davies, pushed Simon to deliver what he calls the character's "towering fury." When Sam saw the last act, he was suddenly struck by an idea. Following the performance, he met Simon in the Green Room bar: "First of all you were brilliant. The production was fantastic. We should start talking about you playing King Lear. You've got to do it soon."

"He said 'You've got to play Lear before it's too late – I was only 46!'" remembers Simon. Sam had always told Simon that "Lear is a part you mustn't wait too long to play because if you wait too long and you're too old, you don't have the energy for it. The great Lear of modern times was Paul Scofield, who was something like 41, which is crazily young, he may even have been in his thirties when he first did it for Brook. Anyway, the point is that you need that kind of energy, just for the storm scene alone."

"That was obviously a very profoundly important relationship to both Peter Brook and Paul Scofield, it was the culmination of the Brook relationship with Scofield." One can't help but draw comparisons between the relationship of Brook and Scofield and of Mendes and Russell Beale.

There was a brief conversation about *King Lear*, but Simon confesses he dismissed the idea. "I just thought I wasn't remotely anywhere near being ready to play it. I know that very great actors have done it in their 40s, so it has been done, but then they were *very* great actors."

About a year later, an almost identical conversation took place following Simon's performance as Benedick in Nicholas Hytner's production of *Much Ado About Nothing*. This time the outcome was different, with Sam being able to allay Simon's doubts. "I thought 'If he thinks I can do it then I trust that.' The one thing about Sam, a bit like Nick, or Howard, or Roger Michell, is that there are directors when you know that you're in absolutely safe hands with them. I trust Sam. I absolutely trust him. I know he'd be prepared to ditch the whole project if it wasn't worth it. He's that sort of person. I won't be in any danger with any luck. It'll be interesting. We'll wait and see."

Before Simon was deputed to speak to Hytner about the possibility of the production happening at the NT, Sam and Simon spoke about which of the building's three auditoria might be best for the show. Sam originally suggested the Lyttelton. Simon was surprised by his own response. "I said 'What about the Olivier?' That's something I never thought I'd hear myself say. It's a vast and very difficult space and it is tricky but I've worked a lot in the Olivier and I've grown to love it. It's so easy to do anything in the Cottesloe; that's also a great space and I'd love to do more there, but there's just something about the Olivier. I just thought that if we're going to do this, we should do big public theatre."

"Kenneth Branagh talked to me about this once when he was doing Edmund at the National – a brilliant, brilliant performance – that he almost felt a responsibility. Although he didn't say it but I suppose someone of his status and his fame, if you can sell 1000 seats in the Olivier then it's a requirement that you do it. Yet there's more to it than that. It's about extrovert, generous, public theatre. Nick has always been very keen on the idea of that."

Sam is similarly enthusiastic about Hytner's policy for making theatre available to as large a cross section of the public as possible. "I'm a massive fan of what Nick's achieved at the National. I've never done a show at the Olivier. I've done the Lyttelton and the Cottesloe and I thought it's the obvious thing to do. Let's do the big one. So *King Lear* is scheduled and it's very exciting; I'm very, very excited about that."

Doubtlessly the pair will have very little communication about the project until they approach the broad, blank canvas on the first day of rehearsals. With a role the size and scope of Lear, he wouldn't want to burden Simon with a responsibility for the entire production. "We'll talk. I'll run casting by him." This seems converse to Simon's assessment that he takes little part in this process. "He's got a very good instinct about other actors. We'll talk about who's going to play the other roles. I think there'll be a lot of people in it that we already know and that we've worked with and we know the territory for the ease of communication. There are a large number of people with whom we've worked – eight casts worth of people to draw from – and if we like them then why not?"

If a particular image is striking either of them at the moment, they are keeping their cards very close to their chests. "I haven't had a single thought about it yet, except for shitting myself," says Simon with characteristic honesty. "I did it when I was 17 at school. Perhaps I'll just repeat that performance – it must be somewhere inside! I don't have a single idea yet. I suppose I might start thinking about that next year." His concentration drifts momentarily and you wonder if he hasn't been hit by a moment's inspiration. What he has been struck by is the scale of the undertaking. "Jesus Christ, what have I done...?"

Although Simon seems appropriately uneasy about the breadth of such a renowned role, Sam is certain that Simon still has "the power and the intellectual precision" necessary for the task ahead. "He's not getting woolly mentally and neither am I. I've always loved the play and I've always wanted to do it and I think it will be great to do it now. It makes sense to me because I don't think it was written for a 70 year old man. It should be a surprise to him that he feels he's going mad. 'Let me not be mad...' It should be something that he's never even considered. Simon is not the traditional 70 year old Lear but he's near his fifties and to have three daughters in their twenties seems reasonable."

Comparably, Sam feels that he is entering the stage of his life when it's right for him to approach the play. "I think I've changed as a director. Clearly, the way that I've worked has changed. But also emotionally, having children and a family changes the way you view certain plays and also your choice of plays. There's no question that my productions of *Twelfth Night* and *Uncle Vanya* were profoundly affected by the fact that I was about to get married to somebody. When you're doing two plays about love, both requited and unrequited, it's useful to have some working knowledge! Both *The Winter's Tale* and *The Cherry Orchard* were definitely informed by the whole sense of having children. The fact that Ranevskaya comes back to the place where her son has died or that Leontes sacrifices his own children totally defines the play for me now in a way that it wouldn't have done five years ago. It's definitely going to be the case with Lear."

Sam's words echo Simon's comments about *Troilus and Cressida* and *Richard III* being good for young men to do. Here it is clear that the converse is true. "*King Lear* is not a young man's play particularly," suggests Sam. "That's one of the reasons why I'm doing *The Tempest* again. I've got a totally different take on the play now in the same way that I had with my second production of *The Cherry Orchard*. It's like *Antony and Cleopatra*, for example, I feel that I'm ready to do that now in a way that I never was as a young man. I think that it's a play that holds back its meaning until a certain point in your life."

HENRY IV, Parts 1 and 2 by WILLIAM SHAKESPEARE
FIRST PERFORMANCE: TBC

CAST

SIMON RUSSELL BEALE Falstaff

CREATIVE TEAM

SAM MENDES Director

At the moment there are two of the great Shakespearean roles that Simon would like to tackle over the next few years. With *King Lear* already programmed at the National Theatre, it won't be long until serious discussions start taking place for Sam's productions of the two parts of *Henry IV* with Simon as Falstaff. There have been recent productions in the UK, with David Warner playing Falstaff in Michael Boyd's full cycle of the history plays at the RSC, and Roger Allam winning the 2010 Olivier Award for Best Actor for his performance at the Globe.

While there are echoes of the frequent productions of *Hamlet* which stalled that collaboration, Simon seems unphased. "It's the interesting thing about Shakespeare that you have to choose your moment. There have just been too many *Henry IV*'s in both New York and London. The most recent New York Falstaff was Kevin Kline at the Lincoln Center." "It's odd to be planning to do King Lear before Falstaff. Though, I've done all of my Shakespeare parts at completely the wrong age: I was a very young Richard III, a geriatric Benedick and a virtually geriatric Hamlet actually. Sam and I have simply got to do the *Henry IV*s together."

"I've promised I'll do Falstaff with Simon and he's promised he'll do Falstaff with me," says Sam, and though he seems eager to approach the project there are no further plans at the moment. "I can't wait to do the Henrys but I think I'd like to do the *Henry IV*'s and *Henry V* together as a trilogy. That's a huge thing, so it's going to have to happen when I've got nine months clear." It may be that in addition to being Associate Producer, Simon will take the role of Falstaff in Sam's recently announced BBC TV Shakespeare project, though that currently remains unconfirmed.

Of all of their future productions it is the two great Shakespearean roles of Lear and Falstaff that are most definitely on the cards. Surely these are the pinnacle of many actors' careers. Yet, with Simon's trajectory for playing roles out of the traditional order, there may be a possibility that we could yet see Simon in some of Shakespeare's other great older roles, perhaps in the *Antony and Cleopatra* that Sam now feels ready to direct. However, as Simon himself acknowledges, the alpha males, like Antony or Titus Andronicus, are not his natural casting.

"He'd have to be Cleopatra. Seriously, I don't think there is a role for him in *Antony and Cleopatra* unless it's Enobarbus which is a fantastic part but I can understand why he wouldn't want to play it. He's not a born Antony, and I have to be honest and say he wasn't a born Macbeth either, but that's just for me what I see when I read the play." With Sam's second production of *The Tempest* playing in the most recent Bridge Project repertoire it also seems unlikely that we'll get the opportunity to see Simon perform Prospero, at least in a production within their collaboration.

It seems certain that these roles will also not be the end of the collaboration. Simon has even been dropping hints about his desire to play a Bond villain, with Sam in pre-production for the as yet untitled 23rd Bond film. Apparently Sam's response to the unsubtle hints was an exhausted breath and roll of the eyes.

Whether or not the collaboration will cross over into cinema remains to be seen, whilst their continued work together in the theatre seems assured. In many ways, Sam acknowledges that he goes "out of his way" to find opportunities for further collaboration. Which begs the obvious question: why? Why continue to collaborate? What purpose does it serve and how does it affect the work?

"I think it's because he's a friend and he's a great actor and he unlocks a part of me that is not unlocked by any other actor. He frees me to be inventive and to carry through thoughts, ideas and inspirations I may have on certain plays in a way that no one else quite does. Not because they are not as skilled but because we don't have twenty years of experience and friendship. It's like second nature now."

Sam is also adamant that, regardless of his continued success in cinema, he will continue to return to the theatre and not turn his back on it. He is also insistent that his theatrical career is in a large part connected to Simon. "Every Shakespeare play I've done bar two or three has been with him. I've worked with him eight times and it excites me and I look forward to it. We know each other very well and I feel nothing but joy at the thought of being in a rehearsal room with him. There aren't many people that you can say that about really."

"It seems to me, if I'm going to do theatre, why wouldn't I choose to work with the person with whom I've had the happiest and most successful relationship of my theatrical career? It seems to me to be a no-brainer. The weird thing would be for one not to want that. I'm very happy for that to be continuing. I hope it will continue until we do all the plays that there are to be done and we're both interested in doing and we're crabby old men talking about the old days."

That seems like a long way off yet. "Yes," concedes Sam, "but it creeps up on you!" he blurts out in a gale of laughter, before rushing to the theatre to catch Simon's latest performance.

ACKNOWLEDGEMENTS

First and foremost, my thanks go to both Sam Mendes and Simon Russell Beale for their trust, patience and generosity. From the initial response to those painstakingly handwritten letters that thoroughly amused them both, throughout the interviews, to the final phone calls from the office or the rehearsal rooms of their latest projects, every moment has been a joy for me. To be in the company of two people who have such passion, commitment and knowledge of the theatre has been a genuine privilege.

Many thanks to all of the other contributors, most notably Kevin Spacey, who was engaging and insightful in his recollections and who graciously consented to provide the foreword for this book.

I would obviously like to thank James Hogan, Andrew Walby, Kate Longworth and Melina Theocharidou at Oberon Books. Their drive, verve and nerve have made the terrifying first-time experience of writing a book a delight and not a chore. I must also take this opportunity to thank Stephen Watson, whose initial enthusiasm shepherded the project to their attention.

Claire Brunnen and everyone at the National Theatre Archive, everyone at the Royal Shakespeare Company Archive, Deborah Lewis and everyone at the Donmar Warehouse, and all those at the Lincoln Center Library of the Performing Arts in New York, provided indispensible access to research material, including the vital access to video footage of the productions, without which this book would simply not have been possible.

Finally, I would like to thank all of my family and friends and my own collaborators at The Faction Theatre Company for willing me on. Lists are dangerous and there are far too many people who uttered a kind word of encouragement along the way to thank everybody individually but special mentions must go to Mom, Dad, Ned Bennett, Sarah Forgacs, Danny Kanaber, Beck Littleford, Danny Martin, Laura Pedley, Simon Reade, Isobel Smith, Barry Stoddart and Paul Thompson.

Apologies to anyone who I haven't had the chance to mention here by name; your support means a great deal to me.